EXPANDED SECOND EDITION

Making Meaningful Connections On the Road of Life

MARK SCHARENBROICH

ISBN 978-0-9826562-6-6

Editing: Susan Scharenbroich

Book Design: Robert Mott, RobertMottDesigns.com

Illustration: Matt Scharenbroich, www.MattScharenbroich.com

Published by Echo Bay Publishing

2622 West Lake Street #415

Minneapolis MN 55416

www.NiceBike.com

Second Edition, first softcover printing. Bang Publishing, Brainerd, MN

Printed in the United States of America.

THANK YOU

I WOULD LIKE TO ACKNOWLEDGE: Our wonderful graphic artist, Robert Mott, for the book design. Artist Matt Scharenbroich for his beautiful illustrations that help tell the story (and paid off his car loan). Friend Mark Sanborn for making connections with friends a high priority. My wife, Susan, who said, "Just write the book already," and not only encouraged me but also edited every single page.

I WOULD LIKE TO HONOR: Our three children, Matt, Mike, and Katie, who not only provide great material but have always given me unconditional love and support. My heroes: John McEwan, Leroy Radovich, Luke Osterhaus, the Winnie Six, my mom and dad, Aggie and Nubs, and my mother-in-law, Julie, for reminding me how unique we all are.

I WOULD LIKE TO CONNECT with you the reader. I hope this book will guide you in making meaningful connections on the road of life.

Thanks for investing in *Nice Bike.* The greatest connection I had with my father was through his service to our country in WWII. Part of the proceeds from the sale of this book will be donated to Veterans' programs to help those who have served so many.

–MARK SCHARENBROICH

Foreword

ONE OF THE HIGHEST COMPLIMENTS we can give another person is that we really *connected* with them. That's because we long for meaningful connections with others. I believe we are designed to be relational, and the quality of our connections largely defines the quality of our lives.

Think about it: How well do you connect with your spouse? Your kids? Your friends? Your colleagues? Your customers? Have you been able to create the kind of relationships that you desire? That they desire to have with you?

If there is room for a little (or even a lot) of improvement, don't be discouraged. In this age of perpetual distraction connecting is difficult. So many things prevent us from truly connecting in our personal and professional lives.

Some people give up trying to connect and live in a self-imposed form of isolation.

Others attempt to connect and are frustrated by their lack of results.

A few seem to understand how to consistently and genuinely connect with others, and we admire them for their ability.

My friend Mark Scharenbroich not only understands the importance and power of connections, but he has written this simple and profound book that shows you how to do it.

Before I tell you about the book, let me tell you a little bit about Mark that won't be on the dust jacket. He is a genuinely nice human being—the kind of person you'd enjoy fishing with or having a beer with, or both.

He is a clear communicator who doesn't try to impress you with how clever he is, yet he does impress you with the creative insights he delivers. He takes simple life experiences—the kind we all have—and extracts positive lessons. He shares such good ideas embedded in such wonderful stories that you love learning from him.

Now about the book: I'm a biker. For the past twenty years, I've ridden Harleys, so I can relate to his opening story in the book. If you want to connect with a biker, tell him or her you like their ride.

But even if you've never straddled a motorcycle, you'll find yourself nodding and saying "Nice Bike" frequently as you read this book and after you finish it. That's because *Nice Bike* isn't really about Harleys. It is about making connections. It is about the things you and I can easily do each day to make meaningful connections.

Nice Bike won't give you lots of graphs and technical analysis (actually, it won't give you any). What it will give you is a way to think about and look at the world that you might have once had and lost, or that you haven't yet discovered.

And if you take Mark's advice to heart, it will make you a better person. And you'll live a fuller, richer, more connected life.

That isn't hyperbole. It's true. Trust me. Read the book, and you'll find out.

–MARK SANBORN, Best Selling Author of *The Fred Factor, You Don't Need a Title to Be a Leader, and The Encore Effect*

Contents

SECTION THREE

CONNECT

DEDICATION

To my bride, Susan.

Since we first said, "I do," it has been

a journey filled with laughter,

love, and tears of joy.

". . . excitement, validation, and sense of community transform mundane interactions into rewarding, fulfilling moments– even if they're only brief."

Introduction

THINK ABOUT THE GIDDY EMOTION you felt the last time you made a new connection with another person. Maybe it was on a long flight home with the person in the seat next to you, at a convention, or a social gathering.

I'm sure a particular experience stands out in your memories. It is an experience of finding common ground, shared interests, and mutual respect. These memories stay with us because excitement, validation, and sense of community transform mundane interactions into rewarding, fulfilling moments—even if they're only brief.

When you truly connect, you feel like you're seven years old again and you've just made a new friend on the playground. Our ability to connect helps us be engaged with our families, be vibrant members of our communities, and be contributing team members in our businesses; it propels us through life.

Our overall health is determined by a number of factors including heredity, nutrition, exercise, and social connections. It doesn't mean we all need to be extroverts or social butterflies to be healthy, but we do need human interaction and connection.

Research by Dan Buettner and a team from the National Geographic Society sought to uncover the secrets to longevity, which led them to 5 places around the world where people reach the age of 100 at 10 times greater rates than in the United States. The team found 9 common denominators that lead to longevity in these areas, dubbed Blue Zones.

Natural movement, sense of purpose, relieve stress through downshifting, 80% rule (which means to eat until you are 80% full), *plant slant* (meaning a diet that is plant-based), *wine@5* (includes moderate drinking)—and the last three relate to connections: *belong* through participation in a faith-based community, *put loved ones first,* and *find the right tribes* through involvement in social circles that support healthy behaviors.[1]

When we aren't engaged with those around us, we miss some of the best experiences in life. It's the difference between watching a sporting event on television or being in the stadium with thousands of other cheering fans, high fiving the strangers sitting behind you after a big play.

We can watch a film on the Rolling Stones, but to see Mick Jagger performing live and belting out, "I can't get no satisfaction!" is a completely different experience. Not only does being engaged bring more fun into our lives, but rich human connections are also important to our mental and physical well-being and can be a protection against anxiety and depression.

One of the greatest lessons we learned from the COVID-19 pandemic was how much we truly need to be connected. Each of us in every age group has a story about how the pandemic impacted our lives, especially in how we interacted with others. We used technology to connect; however, I can't tell you how many times I heard people say, "I am just, like, *soooooo* Zoomed out!" We need human connections, especially face to face.

One of the silver linings of the dark pandemic cloud was how essential workers suddenly felt recognized, acknowledged, and validated. Grocery store clerks were treated like humans who mattered instead of vending machines scanning food on a conveyor. Delivery

[1] Buettner D. *The Blue Zones: 9 Lessons for Living Longer from the People Who've Lived the Longest.* Washington, DC: National Geographic Society, 2008.

people were given a huge thank you when they rang the doorbell and brought a package or a pizza to someone's home.

Our son Matt and his wife, Kate, used to live in Brooklyn across the street from a trauma center. It was ground zero at the height of the pandemic. A large refrigerator truck that served as a morgue was stationed in front of the hospital and was a grim reminder of the loss of human life. Yet at 7 p.m. every evening, Matt, Kate, and all the neighbors opened their apartment windows and banged their pots and pans together in a chorus of appreciation for all of the first responders and medical professionals.

"In the future, everyone will be world-famous for 15 minutes." That statement is usually attributed to iconic artist Andy Warhol, although Rachel Nuwer of Smithsonianmag.com discovered that he may not have been the one who said it. Photographer Nat Finkelstein insists that he made the remark in reply to something Warhol said about everyone wanting to be famous, quipping, "Yeah, for about 15 minutes, Andy."

Whether it was Warhol or Finkelstein doesn't matter as much as how true the statement is. With the inception of reality TV and social media, people have become obsessed with the idea of going virtual, having a ton of likes or having their posts being shared. A 16 year old doing a couple of dance moves can claim to have a million followers on Tik Tok. That sure beats my claim of having a pen pal in Finland at the age of 16.

What does this mean to us? I believe there is a huge desire to be acknowledged, honored, and validated. We imagine it moves us from a nobody to a somebody. We imagine it gives us dignity and respect.

What if instead of constantly yearning for validation, we were the ones who validated others? When we direct our attention to others instead of trying so hard to shine the light on ourselves, we make a meaningful connection. It is often said that those who teach will learn more than their students. It is called the protégé effect, where teaching others can help you learn material that you need to learn yourself.

If you want to make a difference in the lives of others, then find a way to be more successful at making meaningful connections. Being compassionate and loving, no matter how hard things are, will bring meaning and purpose to your own journey. As Eleanor Roosevelt said, "It is better to light a candle than curse the darkness." As we validate others, we light a candle of dignity for that person.

I've discovered a solid concept that can help individuals and organizations jump-start their engagement and ignite their ability to make a difference in the lives of others. It came to me when I was in a beige Ford Taurus rental car and was suddenly surrounded by half a million Harley-Davidson bikers. As I walked through the crowd of bikers, I kept hearing Harley riders complimenting each other: "Nice Bike!" These two simple words, supported by the actions of acknowledging, honoring, and connecting, impact the lives of others. When we focus on others instead of ourselves, when we notice someone else's bike instead of just polishing our own chrome, we make a connection.

Take a trip with me as I share stories from my life with you. Stories that you can easily identify with in your own life. As President John Kennedy said, "We recognize that what unites us is greater than what divides us." Let's find ways to unite, validate, and show respect for each other. Let's make the world just a little bit better, one "Nice Bike!" at a time.

With insights, stories, and humor, I hope to fuel your desire to serve others and put you on the fast track to a fun journey.

Black Leather, Half a Million Bikers, and Two Words That Changed My Life

I've never been on a Harley-Davidson motorcycle. I've never dreamed of owning a Harley-Davidson. I guess I've always thought they were cool, but I've never thought of myself as a Harley kind of guy.

But that day, in my beige Ford Taurus rental car, I *wanted a Harley.* I wanted to be a part of that Harley-Davidson experience. I wanted to see my bride, Susan, in black leather on the back of a Harley. (Okay, maybe that's a different issue . . .)

It was the last week of August. I'd taken a flight from our home in Minneapolis to Milwaukee to give a speech to a group in Neenah, Wisconsin. Neenah is a wonderful Midwestern town known for, among other things, making manhole covers.

While we were in the air, I noticed a lot of the passengers wearing Harley-Davidson motorcycle logos on their clothing. I heard British, German, and Japanese accents on the flight, and I saw plenty of black leather jackets, red bandannas, and tattoos.

After we'd landed, I jumped into my rental car and hit the freeways of Milwaukee. Only then did I realize the full extent of what was happening: I was surrounded by thousands of Harley-Davidson bikers on the road. There were hundreds of signs in all directions that said, "We Love Harley!" "Harley Rocks!" and "Welcome Bikers!"

Passing the Harley-Davidson factory, I saw the biggest sign yet: "Welcome Home!"

It was the 100th anniversary celebration of Harley-Davidson, and I was in Milwaukee, the home of Harley-Davidson. All I could think was, "How cool would it be to have a Harley and be a part of this event?"

Let's say you're a Harley-Davidson biker. You make the trip to that worldwide gathering to celebrate the 100th anniversary of a great American brand. You turn your vivid black Dyna Wide Glide with lots of chrome onto the streets of Milwaukee. You pull into a parking spot next to a group of your fellow bikers, and you get off your bike. You are standing next to your Harley when a stranger walks by, glances at you, and then checks out your bike. What words does that stranger say to make your weekend?

Not: "Where are you from?"

Not: "How long have you been riding?"

And not: "Did you know that Geico can save you 15% on your insurance?"

No, they just glance over and say two words: *"Nice Bike."*

And you find yourself beaming proudly next to your Harley that day in Wisconsin.

To understand the importance of this, let me tell you about a lecture I heard in my Psychology 101 class at St. Cloud State University in my hometown of St. Cloud, Minnesota. I don't remember the professor's name, but I do remember what he said.

The professor drew a pyramid on the chalkboard and talked about Abraham Maslow's hierarchy of needs. The basic needs are food, water, shelter, safety, and security. Once you fulfill those basic needs, you move up to a big-screen TV, free cable, and at the top of the pyramid—cheese. Well, that may not be exactly right, but it went something like that.

As I drove my rental car that day—surrounded by thousands of Harley-Davidson riders and their bikes—that lecture came back to me. And when I saw people on an overpass waving their affirmations at the Harley riders, and the bikers nodding and smiling at one another, I realized that once our basic needs are met, we all have two core needs.

Number one: We need to belong—to a family, a race of people, a tribe, a village, a faith community, a group of fishing buddies, Delta Sigma Theta sorority, a great company, a united team, Mrs. Crane's third-period English class, or a H.O.G. Chapter (Harley Owners Group).

We all need to feel connected. We need to be a part of something beyond ourselves.

Number two: We need to hear, "Nice Bike," which translates to "I see you, I hear you, I appreciate you. This world, this organization, or this community is a better place because you're in it."

Nice Bike. It's a gold star on your paper in elementary school. It's an invitation to sit at a lunch table in middle school. It's the high school teacher remembering your name on the second day of classes. It's a smile from a stranger. It's a supervisor taking the time to tell you how much you mean to an organization.

Nice Bike. It's going out of your way to let people know that they matter. It's treating people with dignity and respect, instead of treating them like a number. It's saying something positive to someone instead of just thinking about it. It's noticing others' contributions. It's listening. It's taking action. It's connecting genuinely with those around you.

Nice Bike can empower individuals to play a more productive role in any organization. Nice Bike can improve employee engagement and reduce turnover. Nice Bike can move customer service from a tactic to a cultural norm that exceeds expectations with authentic customer interactions. Nice Bike can help foster relationships in schools that can lead to a richer environment and higher academic achievement.

Two Powerful Words, Three Powerful Actions

The power of the two words *Nice Bike* derives from three powerful actions: acknowledge, honor, and connect. Using Nice Bike to perform these actions provides you with an amazing tool that will transform you and your team into a positive and productive unit.

1. ACKNOWLEDGE

Nice Bike acknowledges an awareness of others. It's sharing a concern for those in your community and in your world. It's giving as much value to frontline workers as to upper-level managers. It's looking beyond the title people carry and valuing the gifts that each individual brings to an organization. To acknowledge is to be respectful of viewpoints that might be different than your own. To acknowledge is to say hello to a homeless person instead of looking the other way and pretending that he or she doesn't exist. To acknowledge is to have your radar up and to be aware of those around you. It's being full present.

2. HONOR

Nice Bike honors other people by our knowing what's important—not to ourselves—but to *them*. It's taking specific action by valuing others' priorities. It's offering a heartfelt affirmation and validation. It's giving a sincere compliment, not because of what it will do for you, but because of what it will do for the other person. Instead of trying to impress others with your knowledge, skills, or experiences—it's taking an interest in what others have to contribute to a group, team, or company. It's noticing those contributions personally and publicly. It's being passionate about serving others, not because of what it does for you, but because of what it does for the person being served. It is honoring others by creating memorable experiences for them.

3. CONNECT

Nice Bike connects us with others. It's creating a bond—large or small—that makes a difference in the life of someone else. It's understanding that there is a time and place to compete and also a time and place to collaborate. It's making meaningful connections instead of always working on our own self-interests. It's becoming a contributing and active member of a group or an organization. It's building a foundation for a lasting relationship strengthened by personal contact. It is connecting by taking ownership and making it personal.

When you communicate the Nice Bike message, you acknowledge, honor, and connect with others. Though you may never know the true measure of your action, it can be life-changing.

Nice Bike in Action

I spoke for the Salon Association a number of years ago. It was a gathering of more than 500 salon owners from across the country. The big-name salons along with the smaller salons were represented. The audience was lively. Most of the attendees dressed in black, and they all had really great hair. There I met David Wagner, the CEO of Juut Salonspa. After visiting for a while, David and I exchanged business cards. Instead of "CEO," David's card read, "Daymaker."

I asked David about his title. He shared, "A few years ago, I had a regular client come in for a service. I remember being very present as I worked on her hair. We had an engaging conversation, and at the end of her session, she looked absolutely great. I told her how wonderful she looked. She gave me a hug and went on her way.

"A week later, I received a card in the mail from my client. She told me that the day she came in for her appointment, she had planned on taking her own life. She had hit some very difficult times and was extremely depressed. She shared that she wanted to look nice when people found her body. However, after our interaction, I had made her day. I had taken an interest in her and made her feel vibrant, and it was just enough to help her turn the corner and reach out for professional help. She thanked me for being her 'daymaker.' At that point, I changed the title on my business card from CEO to Daymaker. It is more than running a business. It's more than styling people's hair. It's about finding ways to help people discover their own beauty and connecting with each person each day."

David Wagner did more than make the woman feel good with a compliment: He acknowledged her as more than "just another customer," he honored her by taking a sincere interest, and he connected with her to move into a "Daymaker" experience.

NICE BIKE, *David Wagner, CEO and Daymaker.*

After one of my Nice Bike presentations, a woman named Stephanie rushed up to share her own Nice Bike story.

"I was driving with my girlfriend across the country," Stephanie told me. "We were in the middle of Montana at a small gas station, when all of these Harley bikers rode up. They looked like a wild bunch out of central casting—the leather coats, the tattoos, the beards. All in all, it looked like a pretty tough group. My girlfriend and I were a bit intimidated.

"Who knows where I got the courage, but I walked over to the biggest, meanest-looking guy in the group, looked him in the eye, and said, 'Hey, Nice Bike!'

"A big smile came across his face. He told me all about his Harley and asked where we were from and how our trip was going. Before you know it, they were filling our gas tank and washing our car windows. They were a great group of guys. In a very short time, we made a wonderful connection. I will never forget that experience."

It's not about complimenting the motorcycle. It's all about making the connection.

NICE BIKE, *Stephanie*

Here is a perfect example of Nice Bike in the workplace. I spoke in Chicago for Encompass, one of the largest personal insurance brands in America. My presentation closed out a three-day meeting of 200 key leaders and managers for Encompass. After my presentation, Cynthia Young, the president of Encompass, came back to the podium to wrap things up.

No doubt about it, Cynthia is a dynamic leader. She has a clear vision for the company, a keen ability to surround herself with talented people, and a sure sense of how to connect with her team.

Like most company presidents at the end of a big event, Cynthia wanted to thank the members of the planning team that had worked so hard to put the meeting together. Most of the time, the president asks the planning team to stand up and scrolls their names on a screen as the audience applauds for eight to ten seconds. That's the norm.

But Cynthia went beyond the norm and gave each person his or her own Nice Bike. She asked the twelve team members to stand up, and she said, "I want to thank each and every one of you for putting in so much time to make this such a turning-point meeting for all of us. Now, most of us know these people's faces, and many know their names or even their titles. Let's take a moment not only to say thank you, but I want to tell you something more about each of these talented people . . ."

Cynthia went on to share something about each person's life. She talked about their hobbies, their families, and their service to the community—something unique about each and every person. Her comments were specific, interesting, and highly complimentary. She spoke without any notes. She really knew her people. Impressive, huh? But most important, it was from the heart.

Well, I've never seen people beam so much in my life. The room lit up with their smiles. Why does Cynthia Young have such a dedicated team at Encompass? She *acknowledges, honors,* and *connects* with each and every team member.

NICE BIKE, *Cynthia Young.*

I experienced a similar event at a birthday party for my friend Tim Line, who is married to Lori Line, a virtuoso piano player. At one time, Lori owned and operated the largest female-owned independent record company in the United States. She has released twenty-six albums, with sales exceeding five million copies and counting. Tim manages Lori's business and acts as the master of ceremonies for her concerts across the country. Lori's fans are extremely loyal, and her performances are always brilliant.

Tim was celebrating his fortieth birthday, and Lori threw a party for seventy-five people at their home. In the middle of the party, Lori gathered everyone together for a toast to Tim. After the toast, Tim said, "I want to thank each and every one of you for coming tonight to help us celebrate. You are all very special people to us, and I want to make sure you all know the role that each of you plays in our lives." Tim went on to introduce each person and explain his or her connection to him. If the person was with a guest or a spouse, Tim included that person as well. He recognized every single person in the room and expressed how honored he and Lori were to have them in their lives. Like Cynthia Young, he spoke from the heart.

As Tim talked about each person, you could see each person glow a bit brighter. It was Tim's birthday, but he was the one handing out the gifts that day.

NICE BIKE, *Tim Line, Birthday Boy.*

The Nice Bike principle can improve both your personal and professional relationships. Stronger relationships bring more meaning to life and more success in business. Nice Bike can sincerely help you enrich your own life and the lives of others.

In this book, I will present a series of stories from my own life that will illustrate what Nice Bike can do for you and those around you.

Acknowledge, honor, and connect—these are powerful actions, and incorporating them into your life can be as simple as using two magic words: *Nice Bike.*

SECTION ONE

ACKNOWLEDGE

"There are two rules:

1) You have to buy a ticket.

2) You must be present to win."

CHAPTER 1

Meat Raffle Tonight!

TRAVELING DOWN THE ROAD, we pass by a lot of billboards and signs. We see them but we really don't notice them as our attention is either on the road or focused on a podcast, or we are just daydreaming as we drive along.

A word you hear more and more about is *mindfulness,* the quality or state of being conscious or aware of something.

When we are more mindful of our surroundings, of situations and of others in our lives, we are treated to new insights. It is just a matter of being fully present and acknowledging the moment. When we are fully present, we can discover insightful messages and signs that will guide us on our journey.

When traveling throughout Minnesota, one of the signs you will see is MEAT RAFFLE TONIGHT. You will see meat raffle signs in front of VFWs, American Legions, and bars like the Hoot & Holler bar in Blackduck, Minnesota. Growing up, I thought this was a national pastime; however, I've discovered that the roots for Minnesota meat raffles go way back, and this fine tradition is just now finding its way to other midwestern states.

For non-Minnesotans, please let me explain the experience. As noted earlier, a sign in front of a bar will announce Meat Raffle Tonight at 6 p.m. Earlier in the day, the bar owner has gone to the local grocery store and purchased a wheelbarrow full of fresh beef, pork, poultry, and a load of bratwurst and hot dogs. Back at the bar, the meat gets displayed on the pool table—at least, that's what I witnessed at my first meat raffle. "Why the pool table?" you ask. Well, it's not because of refrigeration, obviously, but rather to shine light on the meat. Food safety is not the key issue here.

One dollar will purchase a raffle ticket, and depending on how much meat is on the pool table, the raffle could go ten to twenty rounds. The bar owner makes the announcement to the waiting crowd, "Okay, everyone, get your raffle tickets out. It's time for round one." The bar owner will reach into a jar, pick out a lucky number and yell out, "Number one-zero-two-four! Round one, number one-zero-two-four!" At which point, you hear a loud scream followed by, "That's me!"

The lucky winner proceeds to the pool table and selects their favorite cut of meat from the pile. There is a break in the action, more raffle tickets are sold, and round two takes place. This continues until all the meat is gone. The prime rib tends to go first, and the bag of Polish sausage tends to go last.

It is a pretty big deal in Minnesota and a true point of pride in our state, along with our 10,000-plus lakes, the state bird being a loon, and the claim that Paul Bunyan and Babe the Blue Ox lived here.

So, you are asking, "I would love to bring this idea to my community, are there any rules that must be followed?"

Why, yes. Yes, there are. There are two rules:

1) You have to buy a ticket.

One cannot just saunter into a bar, make one's way over to the pool table, grab some meat, and walk away. If you want to play, you have to buy a ticket.

2) You must be present to win.

You can't stop at off at the bar on the way home, give Lenny the bartender $5 and say, "Hey, Lenny, I'll take five meat raffle tickets, but I can't stay, so if I win, select a choice piece of meat and have it couriered to my house." Come on, now. The joy of meat raffles is being a part of the experience with your fellow bar mates and sitting on the edge of your bar stool in high anticipation during each and every round of the raffle.

In the world of Nice Bike, of truly connecting with others, I believe these two rules will serve you rather well:

1) You have to buy a ticket.

The United States of America is an amazing country because men and women before us "bought a ticket." From the Halls of Montezuma to the Shores of Tripoli. From a bridge in Selma, Alabama to a Woolworth's lunch counter in Greensboro, North Carolina, men and women spoke up while others were silent. They took action while others watched and waited. They sent their sons and daughters to foreign lands, never for the purpose of conquest but to free those who were held captive. All of this was done at a high cost of human lives and sacrifice.

They built communities, schools, places of worship, and businesses. They gave their talent, time, effort and heart to make the world a better place. We have so much to be thankful for because so many before us paid the price of our freedom and way of life.

If you want something in this world, you have to buy a ticket. You have to earn it. You have to sacrifice, work, put in the effort, and find a way to give your best to truly earn your way in this world.

Those who wait for something good to happen in their lives end up waiting their entire lives. Those who work hard and earn their way often reap the rewards.

2) You must be present to win.

I am not the first one on this soap box, but I will join the chorus of voices advising all of us to use our smart phones wisely in order to connect more fully with others. A hammer can drive a nail and build a home, but it can also smash into your finger and cause a great deal of pain. I believe that the overuse of smart phones is causing the same pain; unfortunately, we don't immediately feel it.

I remember the time I walked into a restaurant and spotted a family with everyone's heads bowed, and I assumed they were saying a prayer together before the meal. As I got closer, I saw that they were all staring down at smart phones in their laps instead of connecting with each other. Instead of being fully present, acknowledging each other and making a real connection, they were all lost in space.

When our children were little, we started a dinner tradition of having table topics. A question is asked of the group, then each person has their time to answer without interruptions, and then it goes to the next person. When they were little, a question might have been, "A thorn and a rose: What's the worst thing that happened at school today and the best thing that happened at school today?" That tradition continues today, and now our grandchildren have joined the conversation.

Our daughter, Kate, has a wonderful rule when she is out with her friends. No matter how many people are at the table, any time someone picks up their phone during the dinner out, they have to buy the group a round or pick up the server's tip. Table time is a gift to be with each other, not selfie time, not taking-a-picture-of-food time, not a time to see what everyone else is doing in other places, but to connect. Kate and her friends spend their time being with each other fully, and their friendships flourish because each one of them is fully present in the moment.

When our three children grew up and ran away from home, our bulldog Cooper looked at us and asked, "Well, can we go out for a walk now?" We took Cooper for a walk past our park, and I noticed a dad at a swing set with his young daughter. She looked to be about four years old and adorable. The little girl was swinging, and the father was leaning against the pole of the swing set, eyes glued to his smart phone.

As the swing slowed down, the little girl would call over to him, "Daddy!" Without even looking at her, still glued to his screen, he would lean over and give her a push. Time would go by and once again she'd call out, "Daddy!" Again, without even a glance, he would give her a push and then back to his leaning on the pole fully engaged with his screen.

Seeing the scene really saddened both my wife, Sue, and me as we took it in. We walked on and both noted the inattentive father. If I had to do it over again, I would have walked over to the young father and said, "You know, when my daughter was four, I loved to push her in the swing. Well, she is 29 now, and she lives really far away, and I don't have that experience anymore. Whatever is on that screen will never be more important than this little girl who is in front of you right now . . . but you must be present to win."

One of the greatest gifts you can give someone close to you or a stranger you come across is the gift of being fully present. Look them in the eyes, take in their words, and ponder before you immediately add your own thoughts.

We have a choice in this world to either place ourselves in cruise control, thinking only about the past or the future, or we can be mindful, fully present to acknowledge the moment. Autopilot might get you to a destination, but you can easily miss some of the best moments of the journey.

If you truly want something in this world, then you have to earn it. You have to buy a ticket.

If you truly want your relationships to flourish, to be meaningful and endearing, then you must be present to win.

NICE BIKE, *VFW Meat Raffle winners.*

“A little acknowledgment can go a long way toward making someone feel valued and connected. As a result, it spreads like wildfire and becomes the norm.”

CHAPTER 2

Driving Ahead of the Curve

EVERY DAY WE CONTRIBUTE to our families, communities and businesses, and sometimes it feels as though nobody has noticed. Yet the contributions we make are usually appreciated, although maybe not acknowledged. I'm sure that today you noticed the efforts of someone else. Did you verbally acknowledge that person, or did you simply think, "Wow, it's great that Joe took care of that," or "Jane is really good at her job," or "My coworker made a really smart decision on that project?" We *think* it, but we don't *say* it.

I speak to a wide range of audiences with varied professions. It has always surprised me to hear a client say, "Our people don't hear the words *thank you* very much. Their actions are appreciated but often taken for granted." A lot of people will think to themselves, "Wow, that was a great job," but they don't openly acknowledge the person who was responsible. Plus, when people stop hearing the words *thank you,* they stop using the words *thank you.* A little acknowledgment can go a long way toward making someone feel valued and connected. As a result, it spreads like wildfire and becomes the norm.

When I spoke before the Arizona Assisted Living Federation of America in Phoenix, I learned that most assisted living centers are plagued by poor employee retention. Workers complain that the pay is meager, the physical labor is tough, and the stress of day-to-day operations is numbing. In fact, it's not uncommon for 90 percent of the staff to turn over each year in the same location. After my presentation, the organization honored a woman named Lourdes Hatten, the facility manager for The Place at Glendale. She received an award for maintaining the staff retention level at 94 percent for three consecutive years. In an industry that has a high turnover rate, Lourdes was way ahead of the curve.

This amazed me. What was Lourdes Hatten doing to retain her employees when everyone else was losing them each and every year? I introduced myself to Lourdes and asked if I could visit her facility.

The next day, Lourdes took me on a tour of The Place at Glendale. I took my opportunity and asked her the million-dollar question: "Lourdes, how do you do it? How do you keep your people?"

Her answer: "Mark, it's what you talked about last night at the conference." "Really," I said, "what part?" Lourdes went on to say, "*Nice Bike.* I can't afford to give my staff members a pink Cadillac or send them on a trip to Maui. What I *can* do is acknowledge each staff member—know the names of their children and what's really important to each one of them. We try to do a lot of fun things here to let our team know how much they mean to us, even if it's just ordering some pizzas, wearing party hats, and celebrating their birthdays. Plus, we support each other. Taking care of the elderly can be demanding at times, but we all believe that we want to make each day meaningful for our guests. Our people are committed to making each day count with kindness."

As we toured the facility, Lourdes never introduced me to one of her staff members with just "Mark, this is Karen." Instead, she said, "Mark, you have to meet Karen. She is just amazing! She and her husband, Robert, have a beautiful son. Robert is a graphic designer, and his work is incredible. Plus, Karen is just so wonderful with each of our guests. They love her."

As Lourdes introduced me to all of the staff members, and acknowledged the positive contributions of each one, they lit up like Christmas trees. They knew that who they were as well as what they did each day to bring dignity to the lives of each guest mattered.

As I walked with Lourdes on the tour, she also never failed to acknowledge each of the elderly guests. She knew their life stories, from John's experiences in World War II's Battle of the Bulge to Betty's "world famous" heirloom tomatoes.

Lourdes told me, "I have always felt that you judge a society by how we welcome infants into the world and how we help our elderly during their last days. My team does its very best to make sure that each of our guests is treated with dignity and respect. We want them to feel honored each day."

When people know their efforts are valued, their contributions are appreciated, and their managers know something about them, they choose to be a part of the team. They give more, not less. They enjoy their work more because it matters. They stay loyal.

Nice Bike. It's not a technique; it's a genuine interest in others and the willingness to acknowledge the talents and accomplishments of everyone.

Make that acknowledgment.

Let people know that who they are and what they do matters.

NICE BIKE, *Lourdes Hatten.*

"A dozen people didn't even take a second to glance in my direction, but one guy whose name I will never know went out of his way to Nice Bike a stranger."

CHAPTER 3

A Flat Tire

ONE OF THE CHALLENGES WE FACE when we attempt to connect is that it is risky. We take risks every time we approach a stranger and begin a conversation. The risk is even greater if the person is in distress, and that is probably why most of us tend to shy away from people who might need some encouragement or help. We believe that if we get involved, their problems will become our problems. That's rarely the outcome. Often, when we take the time to acknowledge somebody who is in a difficult situation, the simple act of acknowledgment gives the person the strength to persevere. We don't have to be responsible for fixing other people's problems, but our acknowledgment of their problems can make all the difference in the outcome.

It was August in Minnesota. It actually gets hot here a couple of days during the year. I mean high humidity, sweaty hot. I had flown back home to Minneapolis and taken the airport parking lot elevator to level seven to attempt to find my car. I did find my car, but unfortunately, it had a flat tire. Bummer.

Changing a tire is not exactly my strong suit. My older brother, Bob, can do anything mechanical, which means he probably got all of the mechanical genes that could have been passed along to me. What would take Bob eight minutes takes me more like forty-three minutes.

I pulled out the car manual along with all of the tools in the trunk and began the process of changing my tire. It took a bit to figure things out, but I was moving along. Did I mention that it was hot? Did I mention that I was in a blue suit with a white shirt and red tie as the August heat bore down on me?

During my forty-three-minute tire-changing ordeal, I noticed person after person on the seventh level of the parking garage walking by, one after another. I don't mean one or two; I mean ten to twelve people passed right by me. I really didn't expect them to lend a helping hand, but each and every one walked on as if I wasn't there. After thirty-seven minutes of my tire-changing act, I noticed a pair of legs off to my right. I glanced up and heard a guy ask a basic question, "Flat tire?" "Oh ya" I answered.

"Could be worse," he offered. "It could be January." I smiled back and said, "Ya, it could be worse."

"I saw you working on this, and it looks like you're getting kinda messy," he continued, "so, I went to my car and got a couple of Wet Ones for you. It might help you clean up a bit, ya know."

"Hey, thanks a lot," I said. "I really appreciate that."

With that, the "Wet Ones guy" walked away, but he had made my day. The guy had just Nice Biked me! He acknowledged my struggle, honored my situation, and connected with the simple gesture of offering some Wet Ones to help me clean up.

He didn't need to help me fix my flat tire. He didn't need to call a tow truck. He didn't need to stay with me until the job was done. He just acknowledged me and connected in a friendly, compassionate manner. And it changed the outcome of that flat tire for me. Instead of walking away from the experience hot, dirty, and irritated, I came away hot, a little less dirty, and renewed with hope.

When you Nice Bike a fellow traveler, especially a stranger, it sends a message of hope for the human race. Is this an exaggeration? Maybe, maybe not. But it does remind you that there are good, decent, and caring people out there in the world, doesn't it? There are a lot of people who are guided with compassion instead of paralyzed with fear. And doesn't it also inspire you to Nice Bike someone else, giving that message of hope to the next person, who might be inspired to give it to someone else and on and on?

You don't have to fix someone else's problems, but you can acknowledge their situation, have empathy for them, and connect with them through compassion.

A dozen people didn't even take a second to glance in my direction, but one guy whose name I will never know went out of his way to Nice Bike a stranger. It puts fuel in our tanks knowing that there are good people out there every day who acknowledge, honor, and connect. I know it takes courage and self-confidence to take the first step and acknowledge the distress of a stranger, but the next time you see someone who looks lost, or needs help with the groceries, or is having trouble with an assignment, take the time to acknowledge their problem. Even if you can't offer much help, your kindness will come back to you.

NICE BIKE, "*Wet Ones Guy.*"

A Little Bite of Dark Chocolate

It was the day before Christmas and New York's LaGuardia airport was packed. The weather was bad and every flight was booked solid. Luckily, our daughter Kate's flight, the last flight out to Minneapolis, was running on time and odds looked good for her to be home for Christmas.

Kate was attending the Natural Gourmet Institute in Manhattan where she graduated with the skill of becoming a professional chef. It had been a year since she had been home and we were all thrilled to have her home for the holidays.

When Kate arrived at her gate, she noticed a young woman about her age who was sitting on floor, leaning against the wall and sobbing. Kate reached into her backpack, pulled out a dark chocolate bar, approached the young woman and said, "Sometimes a piece of chocolate can help." Kate smiled at the stranger and then went over to board her departing flight.

Sitting in the middle seat, halfway back in the crammed plane, Kate noticed the last passenger to board the flight was the same young woman who was sobbing. Sure enough, the woman sat down in the last seat on the flight, the middle seat right in front of Kate. As she sat down she didn't even notice that she was sitting in front of Kate.

The young woman turned to the passenger next to her and said, "I can't believe I got on this flight! My flight this morning was canceled so I was put on standby on a bunch of other flights and all of them were full. I haven't been home forever and it looked like I was going to spend Christmas by myself and miss my family."

"I was so sad and crying because it looked like I wasn't going to make this flight either when all of a sudden this Christmas angel walked up to me, gave me a chocolate bar and said, "Sometimes a piece of chocolate helps a little bit." She was so sweet!! It lifted my spirits and now here I am on my way home. What a day!"

Kate overheard the entire conversation but didn't say a word. Sometimes you don't need to fix someone else's problem or delve into what the issue is. Sometimes you just need to have some empathy, acknowledge that person and show that you care.

NICE BIKE, *Christmas angel.*

"If you want to truly connect with people, step away from your table, your office, or your position and acknowledge people with your attention, time, and service."

CHAPTER 4

Get off the Bike

THE BEST LEADERS ACKNOWLEDGE the wants and needs of the people they are leading. They adapt their actions to different situations. Whether it's in your school, in your business, or in your community, you have to look to the people you are leading and serving to discover the right way to acknowledge them. Remember that acknowledgment is just the first step toward connection, the first step in the Nice Bike principle, and if you don't understand the people you are trying to connect with, be it employees or customers or friends, you'll have a difficult time making that connection.

Throughout the years, I have done a lot of work with high school student leaders on how they can create a school culture where more students feel truly connected. I have learned some of my greatest lessons on leadership from the students themselves. One of the lessons I learned was during a question and answer session. A student cited the problem they were having increasing the number of people who attended school dances. I discovered early on that when you, the facilitator, are clueless, you turn to the audience and ask, "Has anyone had any success with this challenge?"

Sure enough, a hand came up from one of the student leaders, and the solution followed: She shared with us, "This year's officers ran as a group last spring. The four of us had never been involved in student government, but we didn't like the way the current group was leading, so we decided to take a run at it. We ran a great campaign, and to our surprise, we won.

"We had an annual dance the next fall, and just as the past student leaders had done, the four of us set up a table in the cafeteria, put a sign behind us promoting the dance, and had a change box and tickets to sell. The cafeteria was full of students for lunch, but no one was coming over to the table to buy a ticket. After a while, we decided that if people weren't going to come over to us, we had better go to them.

"We picked up the cash box and tickets and took the sign off the wall. Then we began moving from table to table, selling tickets and telling people that everyone was going to the dance and that they had better grab a ticket before it was sold out. We sold a ton of tickets, and the dance was packed. We learned that just because last year's group did it one way, we didn't have to. If you want to sell tickets and increase attendance, stop waiting for people to come to your table and start going to theirs."

These four leaders successfully connected with the student body because they acknowledged the old way of selling dance tickets wasn't working. They switched gears, and instead of waiting for buyers to come to them, they went to the buyers.

Acknowledgment means being more aware of others. Instead of walking right by someone or treating people routinely, as if they were in an assembly line, make an effort to get off your bike—away from your table, your booth, or your office. Take the opportunity to interact with and acknowledge people on their terms.

We have done business in the same neighborhood bank for twenty years. One of its best assets is that it is in close proximity to our home and we can walk the dog to our bank. Bonus.

I would say it's a good bank but not a great bank. A few of the tellers recognize either my wife Susan or myself. Waiting in line, I always notice the people in the offices surrounding the teller area. I guess they are all "Vice President of Something or Other." In my twenty years of banking there, I have never had one of these officers leave their office, walk over to me (or anyone else), introduce themselves, acknowledge me as a customer, honor my loyalty, and connect with me as the neighborhood banker they advertise themselves to be. Nice Bike? I don't think so.

I am sure the people in the corner offices are extremely busy. However, if the officers acknowledged two customers a day, they really would be the neighborhood bank they want to be known as. All it would take is a couple of Nice Bikes.

A great example of this can be seen in a resort on Gull Lake in northern Minnesota called Cragun's, established by Merrill and Louise Cragun. It opened in 1941 with six cabins, and it now has 280 units and more than 300 employees. Cragun's is currently being managed by the founders' seventy-year-old son, Dutch, and his wife, Irma. It is a classic Minnesota lodge experience with a world-class golf course. Cragun's also has a conference center where I spoke at a luncheon event.

The wait staff was busy serving, busing tables, and pouring coffee for a crowd of 200 people. I noticed the name tag on one older server pouring my coffee. It read Dutch. I asked the client running the meeting if the server who had just poured my coffee could be Dutch, the owner.

"It sure is," the client said. "Dutch and I worked on every detail of putting this meeting together. He was absolutely wonderful to work with during the entire planning process." I said to the guy, "I don't know, but if I had a large resort with my name on it, I'm not sure if I would be pouring coffee at a banquet."

The client smiled at me and said, "Maybe that's why he is pouring the coffee, because the lodge does have his name on it."

After my speech, I made an effort to introduce myself to Dutch Cragun. He has a smile that can warm up a room, and a heart driven by service to others. I told Dutch how impressed I was that, as the owner of the lodge, he was still willing to work as one of the servers at the meal.

Dutch shared with me, "There are three reasons I keep pouring coffee. First, I want to model customer service for all my employees. No job is too big or too small for any of us here at the resort. Second, it really helps me keep in touch with our guests. You get more immediate feedback than you ever would on a customer survey sheet. Third, and most important, I love connecting with my customers and employees. It's just fun to bring a smile to someone's day."

Dutch Cragun really gets it. He doesn't spend all his time in the front office; he makes time for his employees and his guests. He acknowledges by joining in and helping out with any job. He honors the work of his employees and the business from his customers. He makes daily connections with a smile, kind heart, and warm service.

NICE BIKE, *Dutch Cragun!*

A Witch's Welcome

Acknowledging is stepping out, honoring someone with what's important to them, and creating a connection. One of my favorite examples of this occurred at one of our Halloween celebrations in our home. My wife, Sue, and I love Halloween. We do it big. We have a fog machine, special lighting, a graveyard with tombstones in the front yard, scary music playing inside and out, and mannequins dressed up with masks along our walkway. Plus, we don't give out bite-size candy bars. If a kid can make it through the "Tunnel of Terror" walkway to the doorway, he or she gets a real treat: a king-size candy bar.

The kicker is that Sue and I really dress up. Not just masks, but the full Hollywood treatment. I usually look like some type of flesh-eating zombie, and Sue looks like the scariest witch that you've ever seen. She channels the Wicked Witch of the West right out of *The Wizard of Oz*. More than a couple of kids have refused to walk up to the house, even with their parents' encouragement. Some of the neighborhood kids who are now high school students still drop in on Halloween and tell us how other kids had dared them to go to the "Witch's House."

One Halloween, the doorbell rang. We opened the door and went into our act. There was an entire family of Latino children at the door. They all jumped back as the door opened. They slowly edged forward as I began asking their names and what they were disguised as and then passed out the king-size candy bars. All the kids moved forward with the exception of one little girl who was just petrified. I guess we had laid on the scary act a bit too thick.

Sue speaks Spanish and said to the little girl, *"Hola, como esta usted? Como te llamas?"* (Hello, how are you? What is your name?) The little girl began to smile, and the two of them started speaking Spanish. The little girl finally approached the door to get her king-sized candy bar.

Sue Nice Biked the little girl. Sue acknowledged the girl's fear and honored her by speaking her language. Sue connected through all the witch makeup to bring a sweet smile to the girl's face.

At that point I said, *"Mi aerodeslizador esta lleno de anguilas!"* The kids all looked at me oddly, said thank you, and danced away. I had just shared with them the only complete Spanish sentence I know, one that I remembered from Spanish 1 class, "My hovercraft is full of eels."

If you want to truly connect with people, step away from your table, your office, or your position and acknowledge people with your attention, time, and service.

NICE BIKE, *Scary Sue.*

Bus Duty

John McEwan is an amazing high school principal. He truly altered my thinking about how to make students feel connected to their school and about improving the overall culture. John truly gets it.

I had just finished speaking to all 1,500 students at John's school, Silver Lake Regional High School in Massachusetts. John and I were in his office debriefing after the presentation when the closing bell rang and John said, "Let's go."

"Where?" I asked. "To the buses."

"John, you are the high school principal. Do you really need to do bus duty?" I asked.

John just smiled at me and headed out of the office. I watched as he opened the front door and kids plowed out of the school. John greeted, he kidded, he asked questions, he acknowledged, and he connected. As kids boarded the bus, he wished them well, and as each bus pulled away, he waved good-bye to the students, and they waved back.

"John, how often do you do this?" I wondered.

"Every day," John answered.

"Why?" I asked.

"Mark, every ship needs its captain. Kids need to know that someone is in charge, and that someone happens to be me. When students know that you care about them and feel connected to them, the results are amazing. They want to be a part of this school. The more they feel connected to the school, the better they perform academically and socially. Plus, the best part of my day is welcoming students to the school the first thing in the morning and waving good-bye to them at the end of the day."

"In fact, one of our big traditions happens on the last day of school. My entire staff walks out to the buses, and we all wave good-bye to the students. After a long school year, it's kind of a healing process for my teachers."

Great leaders are often on the front line acknowledging, honoring, and connecting with those they serve—whether it's in a high school, a community, or a business.

NICE BIKE, *Principal John McEwan.*

"... you didn't care about your zip code,

country of origin, or your status.

All you acknowledged was a beautiful child."

CHAPTER 5

Kissed Any Rearview Mirrors Lately?

I WANT YOU TO TAKE A MOMENT and think about something you did this week that was really exceptional—either because you contributed something and did it well or because you made someone else feel happy or encouraged. We all have these moments, but we rarely take the time to acknowledge the uniquely wonderful things we offer the world. We spend too much time comparing ourselves to others and too little time acknowledging our own abilities. It's important to celebrate who we are and the amazing gifts we each have to offer, and not focus on how we compare with those around us. When we can do this, we'll find that it's a lot easier to acknowledge others, too.

It was 11:26 a.m. The doctor told my wife, Sue, to give it one more good push, and we'd see our first baby. Sue dug her fingertips into my hand, let out a primal scream, and our baby was born. Okay, there was a lot more to it, but you get the gist.

"It's a boy!" proclaimed the doctor. "Would you like to cut the umbilical cord?"

"Um, no . . . go right ahead," I responded.

In time, they wrapped our little boy in a blanket and handed him to Sue, who looked him in the eyes and said, "Hello, Matt. I'm your mom, and this is your dad." Our life was forever changed.

We left the delivery room and wheeled down to our hospital room. Shortly after we settled in, Sue's parents, Jerry and Julie, came to visit. As Julie held her first grandchild, I asked her the classic son-in-law question: "Hey, Julie, who do you think he looks like?"

She said, "Oh, I think he looks just like Matt. Doesn't he? Just like Matt."

I got it.

Matt didn't look like Sue, his grandparents, or me—he was and is an original in every sense. It was at that moment that I really began to acknowledge how unique we all are and how much each of us has to offer.

Here's one way to see this in action: Watch babies.

When they look into mirrors, babies have no idea they're looking at themselves, at least not for the first eight months or so. Maybe they think they see a plant or a screen saver or another little kid. They're clueless about the reflected image. Then, something happens around eight months, and a baby begins to realize that the image in the mirror is actually them.

All of a sudden, a lightbulb goes off. There's a look of wonderment in their eyes. They love what they see! "Hey, that's me!" They have a full-hearted moment of unconditional love. And what do they do? They lean forward, touch the mirror, and give their reflection a big kiss.

All of us kissed mirrors when we were babies . . . *yes, all of us!*

And when you kissed your reflection in the mirror, you didn't care about your skin color or the shape of your eyes. Every day was a good hair day, and your hips were just fine, thank you. You didn't care about your zip code, your country of origin, or your status. All you acknowledged was a beautiful child.

So, did you kiss the mirror this morning? I'll bet you didn't, and I'm not necessarily suggesting that you do (at least not in front of others). If you're like most people, you found your way to the bathroom, turned on the light, looked in the mirror, and thought, "You'd better go back to bed, my friend. You're not done cooking yet."

What changed between that baby who appreciates their reflection and the person who now looks into the mirror and only sees what's missing or what's wrong? What happened to the children we were in first grade, who were so excited to participate that we raised our hands and waved them frantically, saying, "Oh, please, call on me! Please, please, please, call on me!" and not necessarily because we knew the answer. Heck, we might not have been sure what the question even was. But we were so excited to learn and participate. What happened to that burning passion to live fully? And when did this person who counts the hours until the end of the day, can't wait until Friday, and is slowly counting the years to retirement show up?

What happens to the childlike acceptance of self and others? When do we lose sight of our value? When do we forget how much we have to give? When do we become threatened by anyone who's different? Those are heady questions, and the answers are complicated enough to require a Ph.D. in psychology, I'm sure. I guess a lot of things happen to us that make us question our value, and comparison seems to be one of the main culprits.

Remember that as a baby, you didn't think about whether you measured up to someone else or whether someone else measured up to you. The reflection of you in the mirror was more than enough to merit giving that reflection a big kiss.

Sharing, Not Comparing

Some comparisons start early on in life: the first day of school. As a student at Holy Spirit School, I settled back at my desk after lunch when my first-grade teacher, a wonderful Franciscan nun named Sister Olivia, said to us, "Children, it's time to color."

Cool! I had freaked out on the math flash cards in the morning, but I knew how to color! Coloring was my thing! I reached inside the school supply bag that my mom had packed for me and pulled out a box of five brand-new, never-been-used jumbo crayons.

As number four in a family of five children, I'd always had junk-drawer crayons, and this was the very first time I'd ever opened a new box of my very own.

I lined the five crayons on the desk, thinking to myself, "I know this one, Sister. I love to color!"

The little girl sitting next to me reached inside her leather-bound, school-supply Gucci attaché case and pulled out a beautiful box of what looked like 5,000 crayons. It had a flip-top and a real sharpener in the back.

It was the most beautiful box of crayons I'd ever seen, and the little girl was proud of them. She should have been: They were amazing. She had every color in the rainbow, including the extra special shiny colors of gold, silver, and copper.

The little girl turned to me and announced, "Guess what! I have seventeen different shades of orange!"

I didn't turn to her in the spirit of sharing and say, "Cool! Can I try one?" Instead, I glanced at her, glanced at my five crayons—red, yellow, blue, green, purple—and thought, "I don't even have orange!" You see, the moment you start counting crayons, you just might come up short. The moment you realize you have less, you start to feel as if you *are* less and that maybe you deserve less. You start to act like less, and instead of sharing, you fill your heart with feelings of envy and jealousy.

Comparing means walking into a crowded room, looking around at the other people who are there, and thinking to yourself: "Well, maybe I'm not as good as that person, but at least I'm better than that person over there."

The moment you pull out a scale and try to determine your human value by how you look or don't look, what you have or don't have, or what you know or don't know, you start playing a game of "not enough." If you constantly compare, you'll never be rich enough, tall enough, thin enough, or good enough to be truly happy. Someone else will always appear to have more or be better, and this will make you doubt yourself. By the same token, someone else will always appear to have less, and this will cause you to inflate your own self-importance or value. The next thing you know, you're on a seesaw—up and down based on who's standing next to you from one moment to the next.

Don't get me wrong. I love crayons, I love stuff, and I agree that having stuff is fun. I also understand keeping score. I understand knowing where you stand in your accomplishments, and I understand the thrill of competition and wanting to be your best. But your true value has nothing to do with the number of crayons in your box. If you place your real value only on things like job titles, the brand of car you drive, vacation hot spots, clothing labels, or the "name" of the schools your children attend, you don't come out ahead. It's a bit like those fake houses on movie sets. The front of the house looks real, but behind it, there are no rooms. It's just a façade with no substance inside.

So, let's say something good happens to someone you know. Instead of acknowledging their success and being happy for them, you find yourself feeling bad or jealous. Hey, we've all had moments like that. When this does happen, ask yourself: "What do I feel is missing in my life?" That's where the jealousy comes from. It means you judge your value by how many crayons you have or don't have. And that's a losing battle. You can't win, because no matter how many crayons you think you might have, Bill Gates and Oprah will always have more.

When we appreciate what we have and don't calculate our worth as compared to anyone else, we're ready to share more of ourselves with others. So, celebrate the successes and accomplishments of others. Share in their joy. When a friend or acquaintance earns an A on a test, gets accepted to a great college, gets the dream job, buys a new car, takes a cool vacation, gets married to a wonderful mate, has beautiful children . . . be happy for them.

Sharing means being a person who contributes daily. It means you contribute to other people's success. It means leaving the campsite better than how you found it. You provide service to your community. You contribute helpful ideas to your team. You give more than you take. You *acknowledge* others, *honor* what's important to them, and *connect* with those around you. It means saying, "Nice Bike." It's ironic, but when you're more concerned with how much you give and less concerned about what you receive, you end up getting more.

Develop yourself to the best of your ability, and acknowledge the wonderful things that have happened to you. When you take the time to honestly acknowledge your own accomplishments, large and small, your self-confidence and your self-worth will flourish—and it won't have anything to do with how you compare to others.

In other words: Stop counting crayons and just draw pictures.

NICE BIKE, *Baby Kissing the Mirror.*

"Find ways to be excited about possibilities instead of whining about lost opportunities. Find ways to acknowledge the things you fear, and prepare to overcome them."

CHAPTER 6

Don't Feed the Bears along the Road

THERE IS NOTHING HOLDING ANY OF US BACK from achieving the goals we have set for ourselves. We design our own road map, and every day we are presented with opportunities that can get us closer to where we want to be.

Right, you say.

Fine, there is one hurdle—our own fears. Of course, we all have fears and apprehensions, but what makes the difference between success and failure in our lives is the ability to acknowledge those fears, do something about them, and then take advantage of the opportunities before us. Too many of us focus on those things we can't control or that have no real effect on our lives. Instead, we must acknowledge what's truly limiting us so that we can move beyond it.

A month after Sue and I were married, we decided to take a trip "up north," as they say in Minnesota. We were headed for the Boundary Water Canoe Area (BWCA for short), a wondrous land shared by Northern Minnesota and our Canadian neighbor, Ontario. Hundreds of lakes, carved out by the glaciers thousands of years ago, lie dotted with islands and separated by portages, where you hike overland from one body of water to the next.

The BWCA is as beautiful today as when the early native Ojibwa first walked this sacred ground. The reason? There's an unspoken rule shared by anyone who camps in the area: When you leave the campsite, leave it better than how you found it.

If someone accidentally drops some trash, you don't complain about it. You just pick it up and pack it out. At the campsite, you cut up a little extra firewood and leave it for the next group of campers that comes along. It's a simple way of acknowledging those you share this amazing resource with, even if you never meet them.

Sue and I both thought this was such a great concept and an ethical way to live your life everywhere—not just when you're camping. Shouldn't the world look better behind you than it does in front of you? With this kind of ethic, every person you meet, every step you take, and every place you visit could be a little better because you were there. Like the BWCA, we thought it was a wonderful idea to leave everywhere you visit as pristine and beautiful as ever. This has since become one of our core values.

Everything we had heard about the BWCA made it sound lovely, serene, and downright magical to us. So, we were eager to get there, soak up the majesty of the area, sleep under the stars, and have a real back-to-nature newly wed experience.

The problem was that neither of us had ever been camping before. As kids, we'd both slept outside in the backyard pup tent with a flashlight in hand, but now we were in for some real camping. I borrowed camping equipment from one of my best friends, Steve, who gave me a tent, a cookstove, backpacks, a canoe—the works.

The last thing Steve handed me was a rope.

He said, "Here, take this rope, Mark. It's really important."
"What for?"

"Bears."

I thought I'd misunderstood. "I'm sorry?"

"*Bears*."

"Really?" I asked, probably looking like a deer in the headlights. "Yeah, the BWCA has a lot of black bears," Steve explained. "You're going to put all your food in one pack, which the bears can smell from a mile away. Just take your food pack, tie a rope around it, throw the rope over a tree limb, and hoist the pack up out of the bears' reach. No problem. Besides, bears are more afraid of you than you are of them. If one comes into your camp, just yell, and the bear will scatter."

"Uh . . . yelling will not be a problem," I thought to myself.

Sue and I headed into the land of sky blue waters—Ely, Minnesota—and started our camping adventure on a breathtaking afternoon.

On the first night, after a meal of freshly caught walleye and some cuddling by a cozy campfire under a full moon, I tied up our food pack, threw the other end of the rope over a tree limb, and hoisted it up. I thought it was pretty high up there. Well, at least it seemed to be pretty high up there.

We were sound asleep in our tent when around two in the morning, I heard this really loud *rrrip-rrrip-rrrip* sound. It was the sound that *huge* claws make when tearing into a food pack that was obviously *not* hoisted up high enough.

My first reaction was denial. "Oh man, that can't be *a bear!*"

My second reaction was hope. "Oh, I hope that isn't *a bear*."

My third reaction was prayer. "Oh, dear God, do not let Sue hear this, because she's going to wake up and know that it's a bear and ask me to do something about it. I'm only twenty-three years old. I'm not a manly enough man to take on that bear."

It was too late. Sue woke up and asked me, "What's that sound?" I confessed, "I'm not sure, dear, . . . but I think it might be a bear."

"Oh no, Mark, what are we going to do?"

"Sue," I said, trying to sound confident, "I'm not sure. I'm kind of new at this. Steve said bears are more afraid of us than we are of them. So . . . *let's yell!*"

We sat in our tent, screaming, yelling, and verbally abusing the bear. The bear didn't care.

The bear had just found a buffet, and it wasn't about to be scared off by a couple of rookie campers. There was a week's worth of food in that food pack, and the bear was determined to eat every bit of it . . . *right then.*

As we listened to the slurps, gulps, and snorts from the bear thoroughly enjoying its meal, Sue asked a thought-provoking question: "Now what?"

I gave her the best of what I had: "I dunno."

I thought for a moment, and images from the movies started to play in my head. I yelled out, "Fire!"

"What?" Sue asked.

"Fire! I remember all these movies where wild animals attack cavemen. The cavemen hold up a torch, and the wild animals flee!"

Sue looked at me like I had lost it. "Mark, we don't have a torch in the tent right now."

"I know, Sue, but I do have a small Coleman cookstove, and I can light it. It will scare the bear away."

Looking back, I can see that this was a really stupid idea. But have you ever been in a panic, only to take the wrong actions and make the situation worse?

I'm not sure what I was thinking beyond, "Caveman hold torch. Caveman scare bear." I'm sure that if the bear had seen me with the Coleman cookstove, it would have thought, "Oh, a caveman with a Coleman. How clever."

I pumped up the stove to get the gas running, and in my hurry I guess I spilled some gas, because when I lit up the stove, it went "Whoosh!" and a huge flame erupted in the tent. Now, not only was a bear threatening us outside, but we had a serious gas fire inside.

I frantically tried to put out the fire by hitting the flames with my hands because this was, after all, borrowed equipment. Meanwhile, Sue was busy unzipping seven tent zippers trying to escape the fire.

Sue finally got out and yelled, "Mark, there is a HUGE bear out here! It's HUGE!"

I yelled back, "I can't really worry about the bear right now: I have serious fire in here, Sue!"

I finally put the fire out with minimal damage to the tent or myself. I jumped outside, and Sue was right. It was a HUGE bear. My only thought at this point was getting out of there and taking our borrowed tent home.

I lifted the tent, stakes and all, right out of the ground. The tent had our two backpacks along with the rest of our gear in it, so it was heavy. The adrenaline rush gave me superhuman strength. Sue was impressed. Heck, I was impressed. The bear? Not so much. He stood below the pack, still eating.

I threw the tent and backpacks into the canoe. We paddled off shore and continued to yell at the bear with no results whatsoever. After a while, the bear finished off all five days' worth of our food, grunted, burped a few times, and headed back into the woods.

We went back to shore, collected the rest of our equipment, paddled back to the boat landing, headed home and we haven't been back since.

What's Your Bear?

Right about now, I'm guessing you're thinking: "Cute story . . . so what's the point?" My point is this: The bear will always be there. We all have our food packs, and we all have our bears. The food pack could be your dreams, your livelihood, your values, or your opportunities. The bears are your fears, your excuses, your obstacles, your competition, or your inability to adapt.

We can live in denial that the bear isn't there. We can hope that the bear will go away. We can pray for the good old days when the bear wasn't there. We can yell and curse at the bear. We could whine that life would be just fine if the bear—the boss, the coworker, the competitor, the economy, Covid 19—wasn't there.

But all that does is feed the bear. The bear gets bigger, and it settles in to eat your lunch every day. Or it takes a week's worth of your food in one raid.

There's only one way to beat the bear: You acknowledge it. And that allows you to stay ahead of it.

You beat the bear by getting the food pack up high enough in the first place. You beat the bear by anticipating challenges, working a little smarter, and finding better ways to embrace the changes you need to make to stay ahead of the bear. It's looking at challenges with a fresh approach. It's being prepared for the unexpected and having a "plan B."

You beat the bear by being a team player—a person who knows how to work with others instead of discouraging them. You beat the bear by contributing instead of being a steady drain on the group. You beat the bear by leaving the team's campsite better than you found it.

Find ways to be innovative and creative in your thinking. Find ways to be excited about possibilities instead of whining about lost opportunities. Find ways to acknowledge the things you fear, and prepare to overcome them.

The bear will always be there.

Raise your pack higher and feed yourself, not the bear.

NICE BIKE, *happy campers.*

“Sometimes the chicken wins.”

CHAPTER 7

A Trip to the Fair

WE WOULD ALL LIKE TO BELIEVE that the world should operate fairly—that every playing field is level. Yet we all know this isn't true. Sometimes things aren't going to go our way—we won't get every promotion, win every lottery (especially those we don't buy a ticket for), or place first in every competition. We can't let that discourage us from pushing ourselves. We need to acknowledge that there are forces at work that are beyond our control, and we need to try harder to keep moving forward. If we fall into the "that's not fair" game, refusing to acknowledge the realities that affect our lives, we'll get stalled.

When I was a kid, our big vacation was traveling to Brainerd, Minnesota, to visit the famed Paul Bunyan Land, which is just like Disneyland . . . only different. Next to the Stearns County Fair, this was as good as it got.

One of the great joys of parenthood is taking your own children back to your favorite vacation spots. You get to reconnect with your childhood and share the experience through your children's eyes. So, of course, Sue and I took the kids to Paul Bunyan Land.

As you enter the park, a twenty-six-foot-tall-talking Paul Bunyan statue greets you by name. (See, prior to entering the gates, parents slip their children's names to an attendant, and the giant Paul

Bunyan booms out a personalized welcome.) We loved this when we were kids! It was a lot easier to impress us back then.

When Sue and I arrived at the park with our kids, I slipped the attendant their names, and sure enough, Big Paul bellowed out, "Welcome, Matt, Mike, and Katie from Minnetonka, Minnesota!"

I was impressed and excited for my family. "How about that, kids?" I asked.

Matt, our eldest at ten years old, replied, "Did you give him our names on the way in, Dad?" So much for the awe I expected to see in my kids' eyes.

The park seemed a lot smaller to me as an adult and not quite as magical as I remembered it. But things got better when we rounded a corner, and there they were—the tic-tac-toe-playing chickens! I had squared off against these chickens as a kid, and I couldn't wait for our children to do the same.

There were about five chickens, each in its own cage. You put a quarter in the slot, and the chicken pecked at some food to trigger the tic-tac-toe game.

Our son Matt took on the very first chicken. The quarter went in, and the chicken pecked and... an X hit the lighted display. Matt picked an O; the chicken pecked again and an X went up. Matt picked another O, and before you knew it, the game was over, and the chicken had won.

"Dad, that was stupid, and it wasn't fair!" "Why wasn't it fair, Matt?"

"Because the chicken got to go first, and whoever goes first in tic-tac-toe has an edge."

"Matt, it's a chicken," I reminded him.

Our second son, Mike, who was eight years old, took his turn with the chickens. The quarter went in, the lights turned on, the chicken pecked, and an X appeared. Mike picked an O, and the game was on. Three moves later, the game was over, and the chicken had won.

"Well, that was dumb, Dad. It wasn't fair!" cried Mike. "Why wasn't it fair, Mike?"

"Because that chicken plays tic-tac-toe every day, and I haven't played in over a month!"

"Mike, it's a chicken."

Our youngest child, Katie, age four, stepped up to take on the chicken. "Come on, Katie," I cheered, "show the boys how to do it." The quarter went in, the lights turned on, and the chicken started pecking. An X went up, Katie picked her O, and a few pecks later, the chicken had won.

The score? Chicken: 3. Scharenbroich children: 0. "That wasn't fair, Dad!" exclaimed Katie.

"Why is that, honey?" I asked.

"Because I'm only a little kid, and that is a professional chicken." "Honey, it's just a chicken."

Frustrated, we left Paul Bunyan Land and went to KFC for a bucket of chicken.

My point? Sometimes, the dumb stuff gets the best of us, and the chicken wins.

How many of us let the chicken get to us? How many of us let little annoyances impact how much we enjoy life? How many of us seek refuge in excuses and denials?

If life were fair, you'd always beat the chicken. You'd get that promotion, buy that new car, or take that fun vacation. But life isn't always fair, and the other person gets the job, drives the car, and brags about the cool trip . . . and we curse the chicken for it.

Face it: For whatever reason, we sometimes don't get a fair shake, and we have to acknowledge the situation and adjust accordingly.

A Sunday Drive

It's not that we have to settle for less in life, but rather acknowledge and appreciate the moment. My wife Susan learned this lesson early on. In both of our families, Susan's in South St. Paul, MN and mine in St. Cloud, MN, often times on Sundays the kids were packed into the family car for a "Sunday drive" which was a common experience for Baby Boomer children.

The Sunday drive consisted of Mom and Dad in the front seat and a back seat loaded with children, sans seatbelts as we as a country hadn't discovered that seat belts saved lives at that point. It is a wonder that any of us survived. We would drive around town looking at all of the larger homes in town. The running commentary included, "Who lives there?", "Must be nice.", "How much do you think that place is worth?"

The drive ended with a stop at the local ice cream store for a treat. Susan's family always stopped at the South St. Paul Dairy Queen. Susan's father, Jerry, took the order from the four kids in the back, "I'll have a banana split." "I want a chocolate malt." "I want a large chocolate cone with sprinkles." "I want a Buster Bar!" Jerry wrote down the order and headed into the DQ while the kids sat in the car waiting for their treat.

Moments later, Jerry walked back out to the car with six vanilla cones. "Sorry kids, but all they have left today was vanilla." There was a sigh of disappointment from the back seat, but in short order, all four kids were enjoying their vanilla cones.

This went on for years until the oldest child in the family, Susan noticed that as she was once again licking her Sunday drive vanilla cone that the family in the car next to them was digging into banana splits and hot fudge sundaes. Indignant, Susan proclaimed, "Hey, wait a minute. . . the car next to us has banana splits and their dad came out after you did dad! That isn't fair!"

Jerry just shrugged with a sheepish smile and said, "Huh, how about that", started up the Pontiac Bonneville station wagon and headed home.

Instead of dwelling on the fact that life isn't fair—acknowledge that it's not fair and deal with it the best way you know how. Take a cue from those who deal brilliantly with the big stuff like illness, untimely death of a loved one, racism, sexism and all the –isms. Do they sulk and give up? Maybe for a time, but then they acknowledge the pain and deal with it constructively.

Sometimes, the chicken is going to win. Sometimes when the rest of the world is digging into a banana split, we are stuck with vanilla. We can acknowledge that at times life isn't fair, then decide to appreciate what we have.

As the legendary rocker, Mick Jagger of the Rolling Stones sings, "You can't always get what you want. But if you try, sometimes you just might find that you get what you need."

NICE BIKE,
Mick Jagger and the Rolling Stones

"When we take a step back, inhale deeply, and try to get a better perspective on what's in front of us, we're able to acknowledge the joy in the most grueling moments."

CHAPTER 8

Take the Kids Along for the Ride

SOMETIMES, WHEN WE'RE IN THE MIDDLE of a very tough trip, we don't acknowledge the real magic that takes place around us. A deadline at work, a crisis at the company, or any very challenging day can wipe away our ability to have a clear view of the road in front of us. We can let the roadblocks ruin our experience, or we can learn how to find a side road by acknowledging and adapting to the situation. When we take a step back, inhale deeply, and try to get a better perspective on what's in front of us, we're able to acknowledge the joy in the most grueling moments.

Just think of taking a long car ride with your children, or being one of the kids in the backseat of the car during a drive that seems to last an eternity. Most of us have been on that one drive that went from bad to worse each mile down the road.

Parents with one child have it a bit easier. The conversation goes something like this:

"Honey, do you have your seat belt on? Oh, betchu do! We only have to tell you once. That's our little superstar. Talented and gifted program, here we come!

"Say, dear, please check the glove compartment and see if we have any extra batteries for the handheld game." "Do you remember the last time your game ran out of battery power, pumpkin? That was a long twelve minutes. That won't happen this time!

"Are you having fun with the treat bag? Mom and I packed it last night for you. There's a little surprise for you to open every ten miles. "Would you like to play some games? States and capitals, world leaders, or Greek literature? What would be fun for you?

"Do you want some music, honey? Would you like to listen to a little bit of Brandenburg Concerto, Beethoven's Fifth, or Baby Einstein Think Time music? What would you like? Oh, I know! How about your favorite? "Wheels on the Bus," Disney version. We love that! The three of us can sing it together!

"Little pumpkin, is your little tummy just a little bit hungry? We're coming up on an exit. Would you like to stop at McDonald's, Wendy's, or Subway? We want to involve you in the decision." All right: affirm and validate . . . there you go.

When you have two children, the ride changes a bit.

"Hey, put your seat belts on, you two. Why do I have to tell you to make sure your belts are on? I should only have to tell you once, not every single trip! You should be smart kids, your mother graduated from college, I attended . . . now put your seat belts on.

"Oh, honey, do we have to listen to that 'Wheels on the Bus' again? Could you please develop your musical taste? Led Zeppelin would be a nice move forward."

"Hey, you two stop fighting about that handheld game. You had better learn how to share! One more fight, and I swear I will throw it out the window. I am serious this time! Just don't put me on the edge. Oh, look, there's the edge! I'm getting close to the EDGE!"

"What do you mean you're hungry? We just got in the car! Look, it's our mailbox! We aren't even out of our own driveway yet! The next time we go for a drive, you'll make sandwiches. When we were kids, we made sandwiches."

When you have three or more children in the car? It can get crazy.

"Hold the wheel! Hold the wheel!" The driver turns to the backseat, grabbing the seat belts, shouting, "Put your buckles on! How many times have I said you *have* to put your buckles on? It's a state law, and I could get a ticket. Do not make me get a ticket!

"Give me the game! Give me the game NOW! *Whoosh!* I'm throwing it out the window. There! Are you happy? When we were kids, we didn't have handheld entertainment centers. We looked out the window, we counted cows, and we were happy!

"There is no treat bag! What friends of yours actually get treat bags for a drive? When we were kids, my mother had one stick of Juicy Fruit gum. She broke it into five little pieces, we each got a tiny piece, and we were happy.

"No, I am *not* playing your music. We're listening to my radio station the entire drive. Why? Because it's my car, and I can listen to whatever I want! When you start making car payments, insurance payments, and paying for gas, then you can listen to whatever you want, but until that time, this station stays on!

"Oh, jeez, you're hungry? There's a shock. Look on the floor of the backseat. There might be some food left over from our last trip. Am I the only one who can clean this car after a trip?"

Well, . . . you get the picture.

I'd Rather Walk

My bride, Susan, and I were on a drive like that one summer day. All three of our kids were on their worst behavior. The two boys were fighting over everything, and at age two, Katie decided that she hated being strapped into a child's safety seat. So she screamed the entire time. It was a nonstop protest scream that lasted hours, and nothing we did to console her made a difference.

To make matters worse, it was one of those hot Minnesota days. We don't have a lot of them, but this was a cooker. And to top it off, the air conditioner was broken.

I'm not sure which straw broke the camel's back, but my beautiful bride turned to me with a wretched look on her face and a voice right out of *The Exorcist.*

"Pull the car over!"

I had heard that tone from her before, so I pulled over immediately. Sue then turned to the backseat and announced: "I have had it with the three of you! I am way over the edge! I would rather walk the rest of the way than spend one more minute in this car!"

This was no threat. It was real. She grabbed the car door, flew it open, jumped out, slammed the door shut, and started walking away at a pretty good pace.

At first, it was kind of fun, because I got to become my dad. I turned to the three kids sitting there wide-eyed and said, "Well, do you see what you've done to your mother? I just hope you're happy back there." With those words coming out of my mouth, I could almost feel my own father being channeled through me.

But then, I was faced with the married-guy dilemma—the dilemma that every man who is in love with a woman experiences on a weekly basis: How serious is this woman?

Does she want me to slowly follow her for the next eighteen miles? Or should I race ahead to prove the point?

Looking back, I never should have raced ahead. I should have known better. Oh, well, live and learn.

But the kids are now grown, and it's been quite a while since I've vacuumed sugared cereal off the backseat floor, washed fingerprints and food stains off rear windows, and retrieved odd pieces of Legos and broken crayons from between the seats.

It's also been a long time since I've heard one of our kids shout, "Look, it's a horse! Let's stop!" It's been a long time since we've played "count the billboards" or sang "Wheels on the Bus."

It's a tough choice. A clean, quiet car that coasts down the road, or a journey filled with things like:

"How much longer?"

"Stop that!"

"I have to go *right now!*"

"Wow, that cloud looks like Mickey!"

"Mom, Matt keeps touching me!"

"I think I'm gonna throw up!"

If you ask our children, they will tell you some of our best vacations were the chaotic driving trips when we stopped to see Elvis's Graceland in Memphis, Tennessee, the Corn Palace in Mitchell, South Dakota, and the Alligator Farm in Florida City, Florida.

Even when times get tough on the road, there are magical and fun aspects of the trip. So, make sure you keep your radar tuned to acknowledge the unexpected, the weird, and even the aggravating aspects of the journey. This is often the best material for the stories you'll tell around the campfire years later. As Mark Twain said, "Humor is tragedy plus time."

I guess I'm looking forward to a car full of grandkids.

NICE BIKE, *road-trip families.*

SECTION TWO

HONOR

"These are my three core values. Whenever I have a tough decision to make, I glance at my arm and the decision becomes easy."

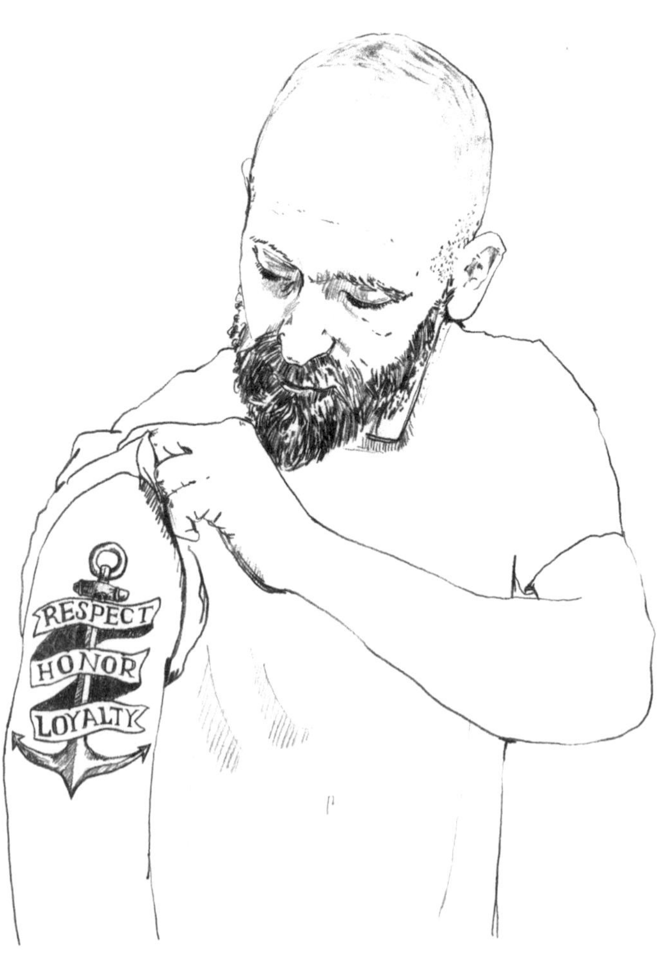

CHAPTER 9

Use Your GPS

IF YOU CHECK WITH MERRIAM-WEBSTER about the word *honor,* you will see it has a wide range of meanings. Honor could refer to public reputation, as in "a person of honor," or as recognition, as in "we pay honor to our founder." Honor could be used as a title for a person holding a high office, as in "if your Honor pleases . . ." or as one who brings respect, as in "they are an honor to the profession." Then there is honor as a rite or observance, as in "buried with full military honors." Honor is also used as a promise, as in "on my honor, I will be there," or even as a social courtesy extended by the host: "Please do us the honor of carving the turkey."

In the case of Nice Bike, we honor by creating memorable experiences for others. It's treating people with respect and a sense of dignity. Serving others. We can serve others with a smile, a compliment, the gift of time, curiosity to learn their story—or any act that makes a positive deposit into another's memory bank.

Our daughter, Kate, introduced my wife, Susan, and me to the #1 New York Times best-selling book by Gary Chapman, The 5 Love Languages: How to Express Heartfelt Commitment to Your Mate. In it, Chapman explains his theory there are five primary ways a person may prefer to receive and give love: words of affirmation, acts of service, gifts, quality time and physical touch. Although this book is about romantic relationships, Kate applied the 5 Love Languages to her friends. She was amazed at how each person responded so positively. Each approach personalized for her friends fit perfectly, like Cinderella's shoe.

The point of Gary Chapman's 5 Love Languages is that it's important to know what appeals to others, to honor others by discovering what their needs are and acting in a manner that appeals to them.

Honoring is giving. However, you can't fill someone else's well if yours has run dry. The best way to make sure your well is always filled is to make sure it runs deep, meaning that it is vital to know yourself, what you believe in and what you stand for. You need a moral compass. When you take actions based on your core values, you make healthy choices that keep you on track—with a well full of empathy and kindness for others.

So what are your core values?

We all have a certain set of values that we grew up with. Values that we were taught by parents, teachers or other significant adults. Values inspired by spiritual beliefs or guided by events in our lives. If you don't have a clear understanding of your core values, you'll tend to wander, and it's easy to get lost figuratively and emotionally.

Not having a set of core values is like having to find your way in a new city without a GPS on your phone. It can be easy to get lost by trying to figure out a map or listening to directions given at a gas station. "Well, you go down the road and if you come to a Lutheran church you've gone too far, so turn around and keep an eye out for a mailbox that looks like a fish, then take a left at the next dirt road. Go about a mile or two until you see an old couch that someone left on the corner—at least I hope it is still there—and take a right . . .".

It is so much easier to plug in the directions and have Siri or voice-over artist Karen Jacobsen the GPS Girl (her official title) tell us where to turn in that beautiful Australian accent, "Recalculate."

I've lived by right and wrong but I had never really taken the time to state my core values until I met Vinny.

I was speaking at a large corporate event in Las Vegas at the MGM Grand Hotel. It was an audience of about 1,000 attendees and the ballroom featured a large stage with lighting and sound. Part of speaking at an event is meeting with the stage crew. They are typically all dressed in black, and they are my favorite audience as most of us see a couple of speakers a year, whereas they see a couple of speakers a day. They are jaded—in a good way. If I can get a smile, laugh or reaction from crew members, then I know I had a good day.

The sound tech helping me with my microphone check was named Vinny. Vinny grew up in New Jersey. (With a name like Vinny, what are the odds?) Vinny was an old salt in the business. He was the audio technician for three U.S. presidents, sports stars, hundreds of CEOs and a host of Vegas performers from Frank Sinatra to Tony Bennet to Cher. Vinny was the guy.

Before my presentation, we were visiting, and I loved hearing his stories. Out of the blue, Vinny asked me what I thought was an interesting question, "Hey, I'm just curious: What are your core values?"

I had never been asked that question before and I kind of stammered with, "Um, to be nice . . . um, to leave the campsite better than how I found it . . . I dunno." At that point, Vinny pulled up the sleeve on his black shirt and on his arm was a tattoo with the words: Respect, Honor, Loyalty. Vinny noted, "These are my three core values. Whenever I have a tough decision to make, I glance at my arm and the decision becomes easy."

I was impressed. Not that you have to tattoo your core values on your arm, but to have an answer to that question is the key. If you were asked that question, how would you answer? Could you state with clarity and conviction your core values?

Those three words—*Respect, Honor, Loyalty*—mean everything to Vinny. He knows what they stand for and how his actions are based on them. Your core values may be more than three words. They could be three or more statements that mean everything to you, just as "Leave the campsite better than how you found it" means a great deal to me.

Those individuals, businesses, organizations, or schools who not only state their core values but also review them on a regular basis and live those values outperform those individuals and organizations who make it up along the way. Core values give you a strong foundation, a deep well of integrity. Like a solid GPS, they will guide you throughout life.

The majority of companies and school districts that hire me as a speaker have stated core values. For some, a committee came up with the values and they are printed in an employee handbook then filed away. Not great. Stated core values must be a living document, reflected and acted on repeatedly.

Some examples of core values from organizations that I have worked with are:

US Bank

- We do the right thing
- We power potential
- We stay a step ahead
- We draw strength from diversity
- We put people first

Great Clips

- We are kind
- We listen and earn trust
- We keep things simple
- We focus on execution
- We exceed expectations
- We make it fun

Take 5 Oil Change franchisee

- Be consistent
- Be passionate
- Fix bad days
- Duplicate good days
- Invest in people – grow your people, grow your business

Cumberland Farms convenience stores

- Never settle
- Tell it like it is
- Own it
- Succeed together

Wireless Zone

- *Care:* We will care about the people around us and the world
- *Drive the Business:* We will drive the business to greater success so that we can do more good.
- *Connect:* We will connect with the people around us.
- *Inspire:* We will inspire others to join us in doing good.
- *Be authentic:* We will be authentic in our words and actions.

Navy Seals

- There are two ways to do something, the right way and again.
- The only easy day was yesterday.
- Get comfortable being uncomfortable.
- Have a shared sense of purpose.
- No plan survives first contact with the enemy.
- Don't run to your death—know restraint.
- All in, all the time

Tom Bauman - Retired Principal, Hopkins High School, Minnetonka, MN

- Recruit educators who are #1 draft picks. "We can't pay you more; however, tell me what your ideal, dream program is and I will do everything I can to create that and support you on it."
- Take away the excuses from low performers. Remove the obstacles from the top performers.
- Continually ask, "How can we get a little better?"
- If it's good for kids, the answer is yes.

Procter and Gamble CEO John Pepper

- Have great products at a great price
- Be intentional
- Be passion-driven
- Make clear choices and be purpose focused
- Always ask yourself, what really matters?

These are just some samples of original and meaningful core values from different organizations. Your next three steps are easy. First, take some time to think about your core values and what is important to you. Next, write them down. Finally, live them. You honor others by bravely living your core values every day.

NICE BIKE, *Vinny!*

"The act of being loyal
is one way to honor individuals and organizations
for their contributions to your life."

CHAPTER 10

Three Million Miles

LOYALTY IS ONE OF MY CORE VALUES. The act of being loyal is one way to honor individuals and organizations for their contributions to your life. Loyalty shows a dedication to building a long-term connection, something beyond the immediate. I appreciate being honored for the loyalty I show. Being acknowledged as a loyal friend or customer is a core element on the road to Nice Bike.

I'm loyal. I've been married to my bride, Susan, for more than forty years. I have been fishing with the same group of five high school buddies for more than fifty years in a row. I have done business with Jim, my insurance sales representative at State Farm, for more than twenty-seven years. My first computer in the '80s was an Apple product, and I have been a Mac person ever since. My father was Old Spice cologne guy, I'm an Old Spice guy. I have worn the same belt for the past twelve years—we have seen my waist size change from 34 to 36 to 38 (hey, this belt is open to change . . . thank you Paleo) and now back to 36 together. The belt knows and cares about me, so I am loyal.

I'm also loyal to companies that exceed their promise of great service or quality products. One of those companies is the former Northwest Airlines now Delta Airlines which was based out of Minneapolis. Some flyers referred to Northwest Airlines as "North-worst," however, my expectations have been exceeded much more than disappointed and I am now a huge fan of Delta Airlines.

If you fly 125,000 miles a year with my air carrier of choice, you qualify for the "Diamond" level of frequent fliers. I've been at this top level ever since the frequent flyer program was introduced. Every now and then, I receive some perks, like an upgrade to business class when there's space available.

I have racked up more than three million actual flight miles flown. These miles weren't from charging groceries and gas on a Visa card. These were real "in the seat" miles on planes. They also weren't from regular flights to places like Europe and China. I've gone to places like Omaha and Wilkes-Barre/Scranton a lot. And to acknowledge my three-million-mile accomplishment, the airline sent me a new writing pen. That's right, a pen. It's a nice pen.

One night, I was on a late flight home and had been lucky enough to get the bump up to business class—and to my favorite seat. I call it "Shakespeare:" 2B. (Clever, I know.) During the trip home, the flight attendant stopped by to say hello.

"Excuse me, sir, I'm Kristi. How do you pronounce your last name?"

"Sharon-brock or Shake-n-Bake," I explained. "It's a tough one. Please call me Mark."

"Well, Mark, I was just looking over the flight manifest, and I noticed you're on the highest level of our frequent fliers—the Diamond."

I grinned back at her. "Yeah, and I got upgraded tonight."

"Plus, I noticed that you have flown more than three million miles with us."

Nodding, I let her know that they were hard-earned miles, "You know, it's not Visa miles with gas and groceries. These are real miles in the seat and not to London and Hong Kong. They're to Omaha and back a lot. Northwest sent me this pen."

"Sir, you have been a really loyal customer to us. To be honest, you've suffered through our tough times of consolidations, strikes, and now we're going into bankruptcy, and there's a rumor that we're going to be bought out by Delta. It's people like you, who have stuck with us through the good and bad times, that keep us in the air," Kristi said. "We'll do our best to make this an enjoyable flight for you, and I just wanted to say thank you for your loyalty."

"Well, you're welcome, Kristi."

I didn't need the jet to make it home. I was flying high enough on her comment that I floated to my hometown. Kristi found out what was important to me—and she "Nice Biked" me. She acknowledged my loyalty, but then she took it a step further and honored me as a faithful customer, explaining how my loyalty had helped keep the company going. Now that's how you connect with a customer in a meaningful way. And in turn, I will honor Kristi's Nice Bike by being an even more loyal customer to now Delta Airlines.

NICE BIKE, *Kristi the flight attendant.*

Here's another perfect example of how honoring someone can create a Nice Bike opportunity. Susan and I had a wedding anniversary dinner at a restaurant in Chattanooga—a wonderful city in Tennessee that has done an impressive job of riverfront development. Susan is a true fan of Pinot Noir, and she asked our server, Paul, for his recommendations. Paul asked Susan a few questions about Pinots she had enjoyed in the past and made his recommendations in a very in-depth and colorful way. It was obvious that this guy was a master in the world of wine. We selected Paul's recommendation, and he returned to our table with the wine. He followed the tradition of showing us the label and proceeded to open the wine with his corkscrew.

But Paul wasn't using an ordinary corkscrew. It was larger than average and had beautiful wooden sides. "Cool corkscrew, Paul," I said.

"You know, one of my favorite customers gave this to me as a gift," Paul said. "I was opening a bottle of wine for him, and he said to me, 'Paul, you are a master sommelier, and you're using a $2 plastic corkscrew. I have something for you, my friend.'

"At that point, the customer reached down and presented me with a box. I opened it to find this corkscrew—imported from France with olive wood sides and beautifully crafted in every way. I was very touched by his gift. I love to uncork fine bottles of wine with this corkscrew."

Nice Bike. This was way beyond an "employee of the month" award or a nice tip at the end of the meal. This was an individual customer who wanted to express his loyalty to Paul. This customer *acknowledged* Paul's talent as a server, *honored* Paul with what was important to him, and *connected* with Paul forever. No doubt Paul will honor his customer's loyalty with even better service in the weeks and years to come.

NICE BIKE, *loyal customer.*

"... the action of real, focused listening
is one of the biggest honors
we can bestow upon others."

CHAPTER 11

Stop, Drop, and Listen

FOR MANY PEOPLE, the idea of honoring someone brings to mind medals, plaques, and proclamations. But actions speak much louder than tokens of appreciation, and the action of real, focused listening is one of the biggest honors we can bestow on others. It shows that we are interested, take them seriously, value their opinions, and generally want to know more about them. And when you actively listen, you will learn things about the people in your life that will help you continue to build a connection with them.

One of the many jobs that parents take on when they raise children is passing along sage advice that will keep their children safe. We say things like, "Don't stick your finger in an electrical socket," "Look both ways before you cross the street," or "If your clothing catches fire, just stop, drop, and roll."

After giving our second son, Michael, a complete safety lecture on fires, including the stop, drop, and roll advice, I asked, "Okay, Mike, in review, if your clothes catch on fire, what would you do?"

His answer, "I wouldn't put them on."

Well, it wasn't exactly the answer I was looking for, but it was one of those moments when you laugh inside and try to hide it with a serious, fatherly expression on the outside. The truth is . . . he had a point. If your clothes catch fire, hey, don't put them on.

Okay, so this story isn't about fire safety, but that advice goes beyond preventing burns. It's also a strong tool for becoming a better listener. It makes a huge difference when you stop, drop, and listen, taking an interest in what others have to share. Step two of Nice Bike is to honor others with not what's important to you, but with what's important to them. Active listening is a great way to truly honor others because it helps you identify what is important to another person and that it matters.

Look into the Eyes of a Teacher

One profession that seems to have mastered the art of listening is the elementary school teacher. If you've ever been in a school classroom for the first five minutes of the day, you know exactly what I'm talking about.

To say that the first part of a school day is busy is a huge understatement. The students enter the classroom loaded with energy and something vitally important to share about what happened at home the night before. It might be, "We had to flush Goldie down the toilet last night!" or "I fell and got this huge scrape on my knee!" Add to the mix zippers that are stuck, noses that are running, hamsters that are escaping from the cage again, crayon pictures that you must see, notes from home about a doctor's appointment, a newly discovered beehive . . . well, you can just say it's mayhem.

If you watch elementary school teachers, they look into each child's eyes as if that child has something vitally important to say, because to that individual child, it is indeed vital. These teachers are masters of the art of stop, drop, and listen. They acknowledge the importance of what each child has to say, they honor the child with active listening, and they connect by taking an interest in what's being shared. It's "Nice Bike" in action.

Communication Pothole

Listening is not a difficult art form to master, but a lot of us never bother to learn how to become good listeners. This is even true of those who are supposed to be great at it.

I met someone who fits that description on a flight home to Minneapolis from Las Vegas. I had spoken at a convention in Vegas and gambled a bit. The presentation went well. The gambling? Not so well. In fact, the only machine that paid out was the one with the initials "ATM." (I leave a winner every time.)

On the plane, I noticed the guy next to me, as he was a real "dress for success" type. After we took off, I asked, "Were you in Las Vegas for business or pleasure?"

He told me, "I was at a huge convention."

"Oh, really, did you attend a convention?" Asking that question was a mistake on my part.

"Oh, no, I wasn't an attendee. I was the featured keynote speaker for 3,500 people."

Well, this interested me since I do the same thing for a living. "What's your topic?" I asked.

"Communications. I'm a leading expert in the field of communications. In fact, I'm known throughout the world as an expert in communications. They call me Dr. Communications.

"I have three best-selling books in the art of communications. I have spoken in seventeen countries and to the top one hundred of the Fortune 500 companies."

He went on to tell me about his three homes: one on the West Coast, one in Hawaii, and one in New York. I heard all about his upbringing, the Ivy League education he was providing for his children, the restored 1957 Chevy he'd just purchased, fly-fishing in Montana, the desserts at Mama's Fish House in Maui, the difference between a low-carb diet and a diet based on caloric intake alone, and more.

He rambled on and on the entire flight. We finally landed, and I almost applauded. As the jet pulled up to the gate and we all stood to get our bags out of the compartments, Dr. Communications turned to me and said, "Well, I really enjoyed our conversation. By the way, what field are you in?"

"Oh, I do seminars on listening."

I couldn't help it. When it comes to real communication, Dr. Communications was absolutely clueless. He didn't understand that to really communicate with me, he had to occasionally ask a question and listen to the answer. You probably have a Dr. Communications in your life, too. Don't we all? It's a neighbor, a cousin, or coworker—someone who loves to tell but never asks.

How Interested Are You?

Years ago, I watched an interview on the CBS television show 60 Minutes that featured Barbara Jordan from Texas. She had been elected in 1972 to the United States House of Representatives, becoming the first black woman from Texas to serve in the House.

Representative Jordan said a few things that really stuck with me: "I never intended to become a run-of-the-mill person" and "Just remember the world is not a playground but a school room."

But the quote that I have applied the most is, "If you want to have an impact on someone else, it is more important to be interested than interesting."

If you want to "Nice Bike" someone, take an interest. Find out what's important to him or her. All of us have an interesting story, but rather than tell your own, ask others to tell you their stories.

I spoke at a large conference for financial advisors. The company hosting the event recognized the "Financial Advisor of the Year". The recipient was given a standing ovation as she walked to the stage to accept her award.

When asked to say a few words, she said, "I've been asked by a lot of you what I attribute to my success. Well, there are a number of qualities that fuel anyone's success but if I had to pick one word I would say 'curiosity.' I have always been curious about others, where they came from, what their interests are, what they value the most. I love to discover other people's stories. Curiosity, a true interest in others has served me better than anything else."

Eleanor Roosevelt said, "I think, at a child's birth, if a mother could ask a fairy godmother to endow it with the most useful gift, that gift should be curiosity."

To foster curiosity, one needs to be intentional and an active listener. Our daughter, Kate, married Patrick Sidoti, a master in the art of listening. Patrick's grandfather emigrated from Sicily, and Patrick is very proud of his Italian heritage along with his grandmother's secret Sicilian meatball recipe, which he makes for us every Christmas. He is an executive with a huge—big—important advertising agency in Minneapolis. Some of his TV ads have run during the Super Bowl. Bonus: He is a wonderful addition to our family. Do I sound like a proud father-in-law?

Whenever Patrick has a big meeting with a client, before he walks into the meeting, he pulls out a Sharpie pen and writes the word *listen* on the back of his hand between his thumb and index finger. It is a reminder for him to make sure that his priority is to act on Barbara Jordan's advice: "It's more important to be interested than interesting." What a great tool for all as a reminder to make sure that we listen.

Here's a pop quiz to assess your listening skills. You're going to hear a six-word question in the next six days. You will be in a conversation with a friend, a spouse, or a coworker.

That person will be speaking, and as they are speaking, there will be an interruption. A phone will ring, a different person will walk up to you, Bigfoot will appear . . . who knows?

After the interruption, the person who was talking with you will ask the six-word question, "What was I just talking about?"

If you can tell that person what he or she was saying before the interruption, if you know exactly where the conversation left off, you are a master in the art of listening. However, if you get caught clueless, with no idea of where the conversation left off, then you have room for growth.

When you get home, do you scan the mail before you look into the eyes of your spouse or children and ask them about their day? Instead of asking your children, "How was school today?" or your partner, "How was your day?" try asking, "What is the best thing that happened at school today?" or "What was the rose and what was the thorn today?"

When you're at a social gathering packed with people, do you focus on the person talking with you, or do you glance over their shoulder to see whether there is someone else more important you'd rather connect with at that moment?

Do you listen well enough in the first ten seconds of meeting a new person that you can actually remember their name ninety seconds later and use their name in the conversation?

Becoming a talented listener is about showing genuine interest and curiosity about other people. That is how you acknowledge, honor, and connect with them. One of the greatest gifts you can give to someone else is your undivided attention, even if that someone else is one of twenty-six students in an elementary school classroom.

It truly is as simple as stop, drop, and listen.

NICE BIKE, *elementary school teachers.*

"Nice Bike is to honor,

not what is important to you

but what's important to someone else."

CHAPTER 12

Dogs, Fries, and Kids at Rest Stops

WHEN YOU HONOR OTHERS, you show special appreciation for who they are, what they do, and what they have accomplished. There is no better way to Nice Bike parents than to honor their children. And when an adult honors a child, it creates a lasting memory that helps develop a sense of self-worth in that child.

If you're a newlywed, take this sage advice from a guy who has been happily married for more than forty years: Avoid movies with cute dogs.

That's it. That's my advice.

Alright, there are a few other nuggets I could add, but I will start with this one. Let me explain by going back to the summer after Sue and I got married. We went to a movie called Serpico starring Al Pacino in one of his classic performances of an undercover police officer in New York City. During the movie, Serpico buys an Old English sheepdog.

This prompted Sue to whisper to me, "Mark, let's get a sheepdog." Now, I would walk on broken glass barefoot to make my bride happy. So, we looked in the classified ads. Sure enough, there was a listing for an Old English sheepdog. We made an appointment with the owners, and off we went to see the dog.

The owners were big-time Old English sheepdog lovers. They entered their dogs in shows across the Midwest, and they had won a number of awards.

The dog we went to see, Maxine (or Max as we later called her), was nine months old and absolutely beautiful. The only problem with Max was that she had bad teeth and couldn't compete like the rest of the dogs in the litter. The owners were selling her for a low price and just looking for a loving home. We were interviewed for an hour before they finally said yes to us.

Even though Max was a beautiful dog, I think she had an inferiority complex because of her teeth. Whatever the cause of her emotional issues, Max was slow to learn and howled like a wolf when we left the house. Generally speaking, she was a pain.

Don't get me wrong: I'm a dog lover. Our current dog, Cooper, an Old English *bulldog,* is the very best dog in the world. He's just plain cool, and next to Piggles (a Jack Russell terrier I met in Canada who could identify and retrieve eighteen different toys), Cooper is the smartest and most loving dog I have ever known.

But back to Max. We used to take Max for strolls around the lakes in Minneapolis. Lake Harriet is always packed with walkers, runners, and bikers. It wasn't just the two of us with Max, though. No, we also had a son, Matt—our firstborn and the light of our lives. Matt was a blue-eyed, blond, curly-haired, delightful child.

Every time we strolled around the lake with Matt and Max in tow, people stopped and said, "Oh, my gosh! Look, Frank, it's an Old English sheepdog!" They carried on about Max's beauty and spent a moment petting her.

After this happened a few times, I thought to myself, "It's a dog. A dog with emotional issues. And she's a pain. This is our incredible son, Matt. The kid can sing 'New York, New York,' complete with a big finish, and he's only two years old!"

The point? If you see someone who has a dog and a child in tow, I suggest you honor the child first. Just think. What would happen if we all made as much fuss over a couple's child as we do their dog?

Do You Want Fries with That?

My best friend, Rick Roisen, worked for McDonald's for more than twenty years. He worked his way up from a crew member in St. Cloud, Minnesota, to the Director of Company Operations for all of France. His job was to open new markets and develop existing markets. When Rick first moved to Paris, there were only two McDonald's restaurants in France. When he left seven years later, there were almost one hundred McDonald's restaurants across France.

This was amazing to me since the French culture is widely known for its haute cuisine. Isn't French food synonymous with fine dining?

Sue and I visited our pal Rick during his tenure in Paris. More than once, we were amazed to see diners bring their dogs into upperclass Parisian restaurants. Canine diners who ate from a special dog dish were literally seated at tables alongside their owners.

Rick worked his tail off, spoke fluent French, and was very respectful of the culture. He did an incredible job of connecting with everyone involved. Rick pointed out a key reason for the success of McDonald's in France: "You see dogs in the finer restaurants, but you don't see many children, do you? There weren't many places in France that catered to families with small children, and McDonald's *does* cater to families. We adapted each McDonald's to fit that neighborhood, and we welcomed families. We simply acknowledged a need that wasn't being met, honored young families, and connected with them."

NICE BIKE, *Rick, tres bon!*

The second key component of Nice Bike is to honor, by creating memorable experiences for others. It's not what's important to you, but what's important to someone else. It's asking because you want to know and then listening because you care. Companies that recognize the unmet needs of their customers are the ones that thrive. Supervisors who know something about their employees' families are the ones who connect with their people and improve employee performance. Communities that value children discover that those same children come back to the community when they become adults. Places of worship that make children a priority and create a special place for children are the ones that grow.

Happy Anniversary

Sue and I occasionally took our three children out for dinner at nice restaurants. We felt it was important to give them fine dining experiences complete with tablecloths and silverware in order to teach them how to behave in that setting.

For the most part, dining out with the kids was a great experience, except for the time each of us thought the other had replaced sixteen-month-old Katie's diaper—which we didn't and she was diaperless—which resulted in a quick retreat from an upscale eatery. Ugh!

One evening, we entered a wonderful restaurant with all three children lined up. We were prepared with the entertainment bag filled with coloring books, Legos, and other things to do while we waited for our food. As we were guided to our table, the one closest to the kitchen, we were seated next to a young couple.

These two had wedding anniversary written all over them. There was a vase with roses, a candle-lit table, they were holding hands, and this was obviously a very special night for them.

I could read their thoughts from the look on their faces as they saw the five of us coming their way: "Oh, please . . . not by us! Please don't seat those little kids next to our table! Oh, no! They're coming! OH, NO! They seated them right next to us!"

When we sat down, the server put a tarp under our table and provided booster seats for the children. We made sure that each child got a menu whether or not he or she could read. The salads were served, and all was just fine until son number two, Michael, noticed that Matt's salad looked a lot better than his.

"Matt, can I have your salad? Mine isn't as good as yours. This isn't fair. How come I always get the bad salad? Mom, Matt won't share with me!"

At this point, I got "The Look" from my bride, Susan. "The Look" meant that the kids were acting up, and it was my job to pull one of them aside to talk about the behavior. I hated "The Look."

I said, "Excuse me," stood up, and invited Michael to join me for a walk to the restroom. Once there, I had "The Talk" with Michael.

"Michael, your behavior is not appropriate for this setting. This is a wonderful and special experience for everyone who is eating here tonight. Do you see any other little kids here? No, you are the only ones, and everyone is watching to see if you know how to behave. You are a Scharenbroich. We come from a long line of Scharenbroichs who are known for perfect restaurant behavior. I expect you to behave with wonderful manners and not say one more word that will dishonor your ancestors."

At least that's my memory of how "The Talk" usually went, although the kids might remember it as a bit more direct.

Michael and I rejoined the table, and the five of us eventually made it through the meal with a minimum of spills, fusses, and embarrassments.

The young couple seated next to us finished their meal, and as they were leaving, they approached our table. I thought, "Oh, please, don't stop by us. Sorry about messing up your romantic evening. Keep going, keep going. OH, NO! They're stopping right by us!"

The couple said, "You know, it's our five-year anniversary tonight. We got engaged in this restaurant, so it's a pretty special place to us. To tell you the truth, when we saw you come in and sit next to us, we thought we were in for anything but a romantic meal. But your kids were absolutely fantastic. They were so well behaved and a joy to be seated next to. We want you to know that when we have children, we hope they're as wonderful as yours."

Sue and I glanced at each other, smiled at our kids, looked at the young couple, and gave them heartfelt thanks. In essence, they had just told us, "Nice Bike." They acknowledged our kids' good behavior, they honored us as attentive parents, and they connected with us by expressing their hope to have a family like ours someday. It happened years ago, and we still remember their kind words. They inspired us to do the same for other parents. So, the next time you see a young family struggling to teach their children proper behavior, why not take a moment to let them know what great kids they have? Honor them with a sincere Nice Bike.

NICE BIKE, *cute couple.*

Dietrich Bonhoeffer said: "The test of the morality of a society is what it does for its children. The ultimate test of a moral society is the kind of world that it leaves to its children." Bonhoeffer was a German theologian activist who was put to death during World War II for his involvement in a plot to assassinate Adolf Hitler. By remembering his words, we honor his memory and the importance of all families with children everywhere.

"As you honor your dreams, opportunities you never noticed before will appear, and you will start to live your life by design."

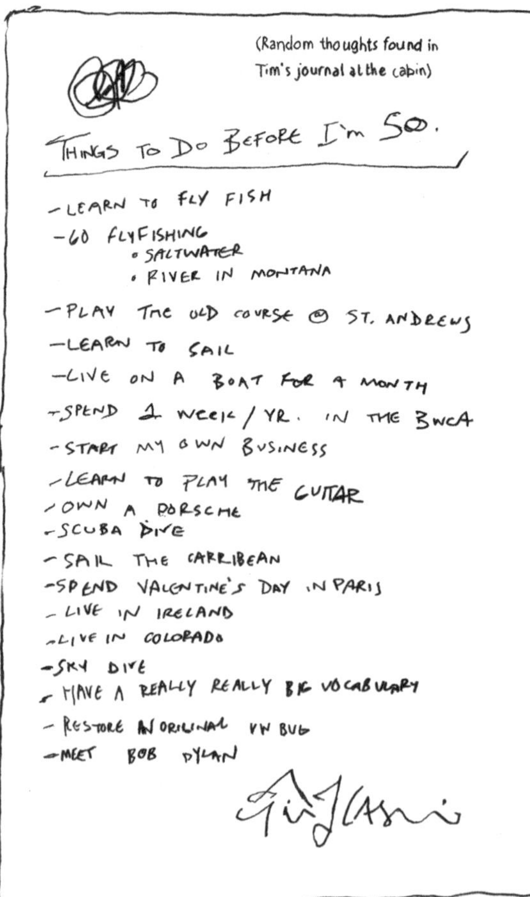

CHAPTER 13

Make a Left Turn

WHEN WE HONOR OTHERS, we are identifying something they value and sharing their enthusiasm. Sometimes those are tangible things, like the great work they did or a new purchase they made, but other times they are intangible, like understanding their dreams and goals. And as with acknowledgment, we must make it a practice to regularly honor our own dreams and goals. If we don't take time every week to focus on what we wish for and put in some effort to move in that direction, we won't be able to make it happen. When we honor our dreams, we build a strong foundation for the future.

The cab driver's blinker was on. In fact, it had been on for quite a while. Now, I'm not a Type A personality, but it bugs me when the driver in front of me has the blinker on forever. You cautiously wait for them to turn, but they never turn.

Trying to be helpful, I said to the cabbie, "Excuse me, sir, but your blinker is on."

"Yeah, I'm going to take a left turn," he said. "I'm just not sure when."

I smiled and chalked one up for the cabbie, but his comment stayed with me: "I'm going to take some action; I'm just not sure when I'm going to do it."

I think a lot of people go through life like that. "I want to lose weight, save some money, call my mother, send a thank-you note, volunteer some time . . . I'm just not sure when." Their turn signal is on, but they aren't making any turns. In fact, they've heard themselves say "I'm going to do that" so many times that they barely notice anymore. It's like a blinker signal that keeps ticking away until they're oblivious to the sound.

So, how can we get ourselves to make those turns when we have every good intention but are stuck going in the same direction? How can we better honor our dreams and the amazing potential of our lives?

50 B/4 50

I had a wise, Obi-Wan Kenobi-like teacher at St. Cloud Tech High School (home of the Fighting Tigers). His name was Mr. Gerald Gerads, and he taught us a lot about honoring our God-given gifts by taking action.

During the spring of my senior year, Mr. Gerads had everyone take out a sheet of paper and write at the very top: "50 B/4 50." The subtitle was "Fifty things I want to do before I turn 50."

Mr. Gerads had five simple guidelines:

1. **Write down dreams and goals that are both big and small**— things that may take a lifetime and things you can do in a month. Include adventures, skills to learn, places to visit, money to earn, cars to drive, books to read, concerts to attend, plays to see, careers to discover. Plus, make sure the goals are specific. Avoid generic terms like *be successful* or *be happy.*

2. **Make the items on the list things you have control over.** You can't write, "Win the lottery," but you can write, "Buy a lottery ticket each month."

3. **Include a number of items that will stretch you.** List dreams that will both scare and challenge you. How far could you go if you didn't know?

4. **Avoid sharing your list with anyone else.** Some people may laugh at it and break the spirit of your dreams. This is nourishment for your soul, not theirs, so keep it personal.

5. The most important step in making this list a part of you is really simple but very important: **Look at your dream list each week as often as you look at fast-food menus.** Feed your mind, your heart, and your soul as much as you feed your stomach.

Step number five has the most power, doesn't it? Think about how much time you spend looking at fast-food menus or sitting at a restaurant table deciding what to order. Do you spend that same amount of time each week reflecting on what will fuel your journey instead of your stomach? Do you spend that amount of time honoring your dreams?

So, why do these steps work? Mainly, because there is something to be said for focused attention and being intentional about achieving goals. Do you remember the time you drove your first brand new car and noticed every car on the highway that was similar to yours? If you're driving a Harley-Davidson, you notice every Harley on the road. In fact, you even give Harley riders a little nod as you drive by them.

You notice those things in which you have ownership. When you own your dreams and look at them weekly, opportunities to reach those dreams suddenly appear.

That day with Mr. Gerads was the best hour I spent in high school. It gave me something to wake up to. It fueled my desires and guided me to achieve items on my "50 B/4 50" list that have been real "wows" in my life.

As you read this, I'm guessing that you might be thinking to yourself, "I can't believe one more author is writing about a dream list. *Think of your dreams . . . write them down . . . blah blah blah . . .*"

I can't believe I'm writing this either. But do you know what happens when I talk about this activity in front of an audience and ask, "How many of you have heard that you're supposed to have a dream list?" All of the hands go up.

Then, I ask, "How many of you have heard that you're supposed to write your goals down?" All hands rise again.

"How many of you can't believe you have one more speaker in front of you who is telling you to write your dreams down?" Groans and a few knowing laughs accompany the hands this time.

Then I ask, "Okay, then. Honestly, how many of you have actually written the list and look at it each week? Honestly!"

15 percent of the hands go up.

"Honestly, how many of you have not written down your list?" Eighty-five percent of the hands are raised.

So, I let them in on a big secret: "Yeah, we all should floss more often, too."

No doubt, the majority of people who read this chapter will say to themselves, "I'm going to do that." But they won't. They'll leave the turn signal on so long that they won't notice the sound anymore.

Sure, they're going to take a left turn. They're just not sure when. However, if you want to live a full life, you need to be intentional, and you must honor your goals. And a dream list reviewed weekly will help you do it.

Things to Do Before I'm Fifty

Tim Cashin wrote those words on the top of his journal and began writing down his dreams. Tim heard me speak at a leadership workshop for student leaders, and that very night, he decided to take action on what he had just learned.

Tim graduated from Orono High School in Minnesota. He was extremely active in school with student government, academics, athletics, and the arts. Tragically, after graduating, Tim died in a boating accident at his family's cabin. Sometime after his death, Tim's mother discovered his journal with his dream list. In memory of Tim's life, his mother and father, Holly and Tim Sr., host a symposium each year for the Orono High School senior class. Their hope is both to honor Tim's life and to give the Orono High School senior class a jump start in actively pursuing their dreams.

Holly shared this about the experience: "In twenty short years, Timmy lived a full life. We wanted to share his passion for life by sponsoring a symposium with Mark Scharenbroich for each graduating class, where we explain the concept of writing a dream list. Using Tim's list as an example seemed to be the way to do it.

TIM'S LIST:

- Learn to fly-fish
- Go fly-fishing
    - Saltwater fly-fishing
    - Fly-fishing river in Montana
- Play the old course @ St. Andrews
- Learn to sail
- Live on a boat for a month

- Spend 1 week/yr. in the Boundary Water Canoe Area
- Start my own business
- Learn to play the guitar
- Own a Porsche
- Scuba dive
- Sail in the Caribbean
- Spend Valentine's Day in Paris
- Live in Ireland
- Live in Colorado
- Skydive
- Have a really, really big vocabulary
- Restore an original VW Bug
- Meet Bob Dylan

Holly and Tim not only inspire others with their son's list, but Holly says, "Along with our other two sons, my husband, Tim, and I are pursuing Timmy's dream list as a family. We are slowly checking each one off, and in time, the four of us will have achieved all of our son's dreams."

Drive-Thru to Dreams

If you haven't put this book down and started writing your dream list by now, I have some great advice for you. Here's how it's going to work. In a couple of weeks, you'll be in your favorite fast-food restaurant—McHungry—and you'll be unsure of what you want to order. You'll look up at that menu like it's the first time you've ever seen it. Then, bam! It'll hit you. A voice inside you will say, "Oh, no, that's what that guy, Mark Shake-n-bake, was writing about. He said to spend as much time each week looking at my dream list as I do looking at fast-food menus. Ohhh . . . ohhhh . . . he got me!"

You will place your order, sit down with your fries, grab a pen and paper, and start writing down your dreams. Your efforts will be rewarded, and doors of opportunity will indeed open. As you honor your dreams, opportunities you never noticed before will appear, and you will start to live your life by design.

What opportunities do you wake up to every day? What gives you a spark in life? What hopes and dreams fill your life with passion?

Using the Nice Bike principle will strengthen your connections with others. Honoring an active dream list will fuel your ride in life with a sense of direction, self-determination, and accomplishment. You'll never leave your blinker stuck on left turn ever again.

NICE BIKE, *Mr. Gerads and Timmy Cashin.*

"It's not enough to honor your strengths–they don't always present the best learning opportunities or chances for growth. You must also honor your weaknesses."

CHAPTER 14

Take a Mulligan

EVERY EXPERIENCE IN OUR LIVES presents the possibility to learn something new—about the world, about others, or about ourselves. To make the most of those lessons, we have to honor the opportunities to learn. Often those opportunities come through in our failures and misguided choices. It's not enough to honor your strengths—they don't always present the best learning opportunities or chances for growth. You must also honor your weaknesses. Face your mistakes and learn from them. Honor the lessons you learn by pushing yourself to pursue your dreams.

I no longer golf with my buddies. I'm not a good golfer to begin with. In fact, every time I hit the ball, I have no idea where it might go. So, golfing with my buddies puts added pressure on what should be a relaxing game. When I hit a ball poorly, they either roll their eyes or say things like "Ouch" and "Oops!" Or they suggest that I change my grip, my stance, my feet, my shoulders, my belt buckle—you name it. So, now, I golf only with my wife or with my wife and her friends. When I hit a shot poorly in front of my wife, she just reaches into her pocket, throws another ball at me, and says, "Oh, honey, try another one." I like that.

The last time I golfed with my male friends, it was a gorgeous Saturday morning. I was first up at the tee box, and I pulled out my three-iron to drive the ball. (I've given up using a driver at the tee, as it usually ends up in the next fairway or dangerously close to some other golfer's head.) This particular day, my three buddies were standing behind me, leaning on their Big Bertha woods with legs crossed, and saying things like, "Okay, Mr. Motivational Speaker Boy, hit that ball. Give us something to chase. Raise the bar. Hit it out of the box. Be all you can be. Your attitude will direct the altitude of the ball."

My self-talk or mantra before every golf swing is "Swing like a nine-year-old girl, only slower, and let the club do the work." But the banter from my friends changed the self-talk to "I'm going to drive this ball one million miles!" So, of course, I swung too hard, barely touching the ball, and it rolled for about fifteen yards.

Instead of tossing me a second ball like my wife, my buddies just said, "Nice start, Speaker Boy! Way to get ahold of it. Drop your pants, and go pick it up." I guess the "dropping the pants" thing is a golf tradition. At least that's what my buddies told me.

At that point, I asked a question that most golfers can appreciate: "Can I have a mulligan?" A mulligan in golf means a "do over." It's a second chance to get it right.

I like the word *mulligan,* and I think it applies to more than just a "do over" in golf.

Whether you're a golfer or not, I believe that we all have and need mulligans in life—times in our lives when we wish we hadn't said something, when we made a poor decision, or when we took roads we shouldn't have taken.

It's important to know when your mulligan moments are, to learn from your mulligans, and to do something about your mulligans when you can.

My fellow speaker and author Eric Chester, looks at his mulligans as "tuition." For Eric, each day is an opportunity to learn something new. School doesn't end with high school, training school, or a college diploma. School is never out, and we need to be open to learning all of the time. I have listened to Eric describe his missteps like this: "I paid my tuition on that one. I won't make that mistake again." Instead of getting down on himself for the error, he chalks it up to a lesson learned, and the aggravation he experienced in the process is the "tuition paid" to learn that lesson. He honors his mistakes and his mulligans as valuable learning experiences.

Most of our mulligans are wrong turns we have made along the way. When possible, you can have a "do over"—a second chance to learn from that wrong turn and remedy the mistake through another action. The toughest mulligans to face, however, are the ones when you don't have a second chance to fix something. Or worse yet, the times when you never step up to the tee box to hit your shot in the first place. In life, we call those regrets "Woulda, coulda, shoulda," "If only . . . ," and "Someday . . ."

Are Your Dreams on Hold?

One big reason we don't step up and take a risk is the fear of failure. "What if I screw up?" "What if I lose?" When you ask people in the last stages of their lives if they have any regrets, they'll usually talk about opportunities they never pursued and roads they never traveled.

So, I believe that every now and then, you have to scare yourself with a challenge. This usually means putting yourself in a situation where you fear you're in over your pay grade—something that makes you nervous enough to keep you awake at night. Here's an example: I was invited to speak to a unique group called the 21st Century Cardiothoracic Surgical Society, which is composed of fifty of the most gifted and successful cardiac surgeons across the country. The meeting was sponsored in part by Medtronic, and I was going to speak at the final banquet for the surgeons, their spouses, and guests. When I say these surgeons are intelligent, I don't mean they're kind of smart. I mean that they're *brilliant.* They're the chief surgeons from all over the United States, including Harvard, Stanford, and the Mayo Clinic. To get to know the group better, I sat in on their large-group session as they gave presentations about their cutting-edge research. I had my yellow legal pad and Bic pen ready to take notes. I remember writing down words that I understood, like *the* and *procedure.*

In the back of my head, all I could hear was a voice that said, "These people are brilliant, and I'm such a dim bulb. I'm so far out of my league. I'm in way over my head. I think I'm going to be sick."

The banquet time arrived, and I talked about the things I know something about—making meaningful connections with family, peers. I talked about the experience of being a patient. I talked about the Nice Bike concept and how it applied to their lives. The presentation hit home with them, and they were a wonderful audience. It worked. Yeah! I have never had a presentation scare me more, and I have never had a presentation which I walked away from feeling better. I had survived. I had acknowledged my fear, honored the challenge, and connected with the opportunity.

When is the last time you scared yourself? When was the last time you thought, "I don't know if I can pull this off, but I'm going to give it a shot"? When was the last time you headed down a road that wasn't all that familiar to you?

What roadblock keeps you from traveling down a new road more than anything else? We often begin excuses with "As soon as I . . ." It starts in high school: "I'm new, only in ninth grade. I don't know very much, so as soon as I'm a senior, I'll raise my hand more, try out for a team or the play, make some new friends, and be more vocal, because when you're a senior, people look up to you."

It's always something: "As soon as I graduate from high school, that's when I'll get more involved. This school just isn't a good place for me. I don't really fit in."

Then, it's: "As soon as I get my first job, that's when I'll have a greater purpose. My life is kind of on hold right now, and I don't have a clear vision of where I'm going. As soon as I get my first job, move away from home, get my own place, and make my own money, that's when life is really going to be fun."

Or it's: "As soon as I fall in love and get married, life will be great. As soon as I find someone, I won't be alone: we'll share good times each day."

You know the drill:

"As soon as I have kids . . ."

"As soon as I get a new job . . ."

"As soon as I retire . . ."

"As soon as I'm dead . . . As soon as I'm dead, I'll have all the time in the world."

Today is a good day to discard your "As soon as I" list. In fact, today is a perfect day to take your first step down a new road. My friend, author and speaker, Mark Sanborn writes in his book *The Encore Effect:* "Passion and discipline without action is just day-dreaming."

So, tee it up. Take a deep breath, and take a swing. Even if you have to take a mulligan, you're moving ahead with your dreams.

NICE BIKE, *my fellow duffers.*

SECTION THREE

CONNECT

"When we keep our radar up

and notice the connections around us,

we learn daily lessons on how to treat others."

CHAPTER 15

A Ride to the Grocery Store for Milk

CONNECTING WITH OTHERS MATTERS. It matters in both our personal and professional lives. It matters on the world stage and in our own backyards. To be a part of an authentic and meaningful connection is a rich experience. You never know when you might be interacting with an organization or business that takes pride in building strong connections with its employees, customers, and community. When we keep our radar up and notice the connections around us, we learn daily lessons on how to treat others.

When it gets cold in Minnesota—and I mean *really* cold—we either drive out on a frozen lake to go ice fishing, or we stay home and eat. So, we love our world-class grocery stores, Lunds and Byerly's. They are absolutely beautiful, and when relatives come to town it's not unusual to take them to these stores for a fun visit.

Lunds and Byerly's have set the bar extremely high. This means that the run for a loaf of bread and a gallon of milk becomes more than an errand—it's an experience. The produce is displayed perfectly, the meat counter reminds you of a small-town butcher shop, and their offerings are impressive with items like thirty-one different types of mustard.

We also love our neighborhood grocery store called Fresh Seasons, opened by the former president and chief operating officer of Byerly's named Dale Riley. Inspired by the quality of Lunds and Byerly's, Fresh Seasons offers its own brand of wonderfulness. The walls are filled with warm colors and art. It stocks delicious homemade goods in the deli. The produce section is packed with a wide variety of fresh produce and the meat and seafood section is a work of art. It's a gem.

The most impressive aspect of Fresh Seasons is the staff and the connection they make with their customers and each other. Everyone goes out of his or her way to remember your name and take an interest in you as a customer. The staff makes you feel like an honored guest, and it works—you really do want to go back, take your kids, and stay awhile. They seem authentically happy that they are working at Fresh Seasons and that you're shopping there.

Getting the entire team at a grocery store—from the produce department to the meat counter to the cashier to the bagger—to buy into personal and authentic positive customer experiences impresses me.

A key reason for this true customer service experience is Dale Riley. Dale knows how to connect with his customers and his team. The odds are really good that if you meet Dale once, he will remember you the next time you walk into the store. It's easy to find Dale when you visit Fresh Seasons. He's the one bagging groceries, sweeping the front walk, taking care of a spill in aisle four, or drinking coffee with the customers in the deli. I once heard a customer ask him, "Dale, is there anything you don't do here?"

His answer: "Nope."

People are willing to follow a manager who is willing to walk in everyone else's shoes. Plus, if Dale is not in the store, you'll find one of his managers modeling his lead. They're easy to spot, and their positive presence is felt by everyone in the store—both employees and customers.

I asked Dale what he did to get everyone to buy in to delivering that level of service, to making an effort to connect with customers. Dale said, "Mark, it's three things: first, I ask my team to take ownership in the store, second, I ask my team to take an interest in our guests, and third, have fun. It's that simple."

"Simple," Dale says. It may be simple, but it isn't easy. If it were, every manager would do it. The reason they don't is that it takes effort on a daily basis to create and maintain a strong culture that connects an entire team. Great organizations have great leaders who not only get it but also work at it daily. And the rewards of that work can quickly be seen when you walk into a place like Fresh Seasons.

Dale is a great leader because he connects with his employees, helps them to feel great about coming to work, and creates a family culture with the entire team. He does this by taking an interest in who they are and what they like, and he values their ideas. Dale makes it a point to Nice Bike them often.

One of the baggers at Fresh Seasons is a high school student named Gabby. Her name fits her personality. As Gabby bags your groceries, she does a running commentary about what she's putting in the bag for you. "Do you really like this? I've never had this before. Did you know that was on sale? How do you cook these?"

I asked Gabby why she enjoys working at Fresh Seasons so much. She said, "It's fun!" "Everyone here gets along really well. Plus, Mr. Riley is the best boss in the world. He really knows us. In fact, Mr. Riley found out that I was a huge fan of Cesar Millan, the Dog Whisperer. Cesar is on the National Geographic Channel all of the time, and I just love him! The Dog Whisperer came to Minneapolis for a presentation, and Mr. Riley got tickets for my parents and me to attend. That was just so cool."

Putting an "Employee of the Week" picture on the wall is nice, but knowing that Gabby is a huge fan of the Dog Whisperer is something else altogether. Recognizing what's important to his people is vital, getting tickets for Gabby, as well as her parents, is validating, and connecting with a bagger on his team is priceless.

Nice Bike means taking an interest in someone else through acknowledgment, honoring them by finding out what's important to them, and connecting by making it personal. Leading by example, Dale has inspired his team to connect with each other and with the people they serve.

NICE BIKE, *Dale Riley.*

"You never know when you might create an important connection with someone that could change your life or theirs."

CHAPTER 16

Driving Aggie

YOU NEVER KNOW when you might create an important connection with someone that could change your life or theirs. And sometimes, you might be making a connection and not even realize it.

My parents were named Norbert and Agnes, but everyone called them Nubs and Aggie. That generation had such colorful names: Bud & Cleo, Irv & Dory, Maury & Helen, Orville & Adeline, the list goes on. Not exactly the nicknames a kid would pick out for his parents, but they were the best parents a kid could ever be lucky enough to have.

Nubs was born in St. Cloud, Minnesota, and his grandparents were from Germany. Aggie was born in Minnesota, too, and her parents were both Irish. Now, that's quite a mix: German structure blended with the carefree heart of the Irish. Good stuff, you betcha.

Dad worked at the St. Cloud post office where he sorted mail for a living. He was a good guy—just not the most flexible person you'd ever meet. He was a classic old-school dad:

"We eat at 5:30 p.m. sharp. If you are not at the table, you won't be eating with us tonight."

"We buy Ford. What the heck were you thinking when you bought that Fiat?"

"We eat fish on Friday. I don't care if the Pope says it's now okay to eat meat on Friday. I am not going to go to hell because that guy changed the rules."

"That's my chair. If I am not in the house, you can go ahead and give it a test drive, but if I walk in the back door, you get the heck out of my chair."

One thing was for sure—you knew where my dad stood on all issues.

My mom? Well, Aggie's a saint, and if there's a hard way to do something, she'll find it. At ninety-four years of age, she still did the laundry in the basement with a Maytag wringer washer. You can only find them in an antique store today. She then took the laundry, hauled it in a basket up the basement steps and outside to hang on the clotheslines. Mom did this every Monday, every month of the year, including January.

Of course, if you live outside of Minnesota, you may have no idea what happened to Mom's wet laundry when she hung it outside in January. The clothes didn't freeze eventually . . . they froze *immediately!* Mom then took the frozen laundry off the lines—stiff as a board—and hung it on the kitchen chairs to dry. I once asked her, "Mom, why do you do this?"

Her response was, "Oh, it just smells better."

I didn't realize it at the time, but it was just one more of

the many lessons Mom taught me through actions instead of words. The lesson being that if you want better results, then you need to put in better efforts.

Mom had arthritis in her hands, and sometimes, it got pretty painful. Yet, in her spare time, she sewed quilts and gave them away. Mom's belief was that if you let the little pains in life slow you down, you're giving up, and there's no time for that.

I can honestly say that I have never—and I do mean never—heard my mother complain or whine about anything. I, on the other hand, whine constantly! When I grow up, I want to be as appreciative of life as my mom was every day.

700 Candy Canes

With five children in the house when we were growing up, mom never worked outside the home—until Dad retired. Then, she got a job outside the home as a cafeteria monitor at an elementary school. Mom carried a washcloth, a whistle, and a clipboard. Her mission was to keep a sense of order in the cafeteria and help the kids open their milk cartons when needed.

Going to work wasn't a tough decision for mom: Spend a couple of hours every day monitoring 700 noisy, hungry elementary school kids in a crowded cafeteria, or spend that time with classic old-school Nubs? She jumped at the chance to be with the 700 noisy kids in a New York minute.

Mom loved her job. She connected with the kids, and the kids connected with her. They called her "Aggie, the Retainer Lady." This was because kids wrapped their retainers in napkins and put them on their trays at lunch. At the end of lunch, they'd often forget about the wrapped retainers and accidentally dump them in the trash.

Five minutes later, they would run to my mom and say, "Aggie, I forgot my retainer wrapped in a napkin, and I threw it in the garbage can!" With that, mom would don a pair of rubber gloves and dig in the trash bin until she found the retainer.

Every time mom saved a retainer, one of the cooks would comment, "Aggie, we saw you digging through the garbage again for a retainer. We would never do that."

Mom's reply, "Oh, these are kids. I'll always do that."

Mom was also famous for keeping Hershey's Kisses in her pocket, and whenever students had a birthday, they always told my mom in order to get one of "Aggie's birthday kisses."

One Christmas after Mom had been working at the school for a few years, I was talking to Dad, and he came out with his usual, "What the hell!" It was one of his favorite expressions. It worked for everything—good, bad, or indifferent.

Then, there was a long pause, and he shook his head.

"What is it, Dad?"

"Oh, it's your mother."

"What about Mom?"

"Those doggone candy canes, Mark. For cryin' out loud! Seven hundred of them to be exact. Every year since she's been at the elementary school, it's the same darn thing. Plus, she doesn't want the little candy canes—they're not good enough for the kids! She wants the big ones, cripes! I have to drive all over town and try to find them, and you know we're living on a fixed income. It's not like we're the Rockefellers. Money doesn't grow on trees! I wish it did, but it doesn't. But you know your mother!"

"Dad, I'm clueless here. What are you talking about?"

At this point, my sister, JoAnne, the kindergarten teacher, joined in the conversation and explained to me that Mom was giving every student at the elementary school a candy cane over the holidays. On the cafeteria menu board, it would read, "Aggie's candy canes!"

Now, for Dad, this was a big deal, because he had to drive all over town and try to find those 700 *big* candy canes. Mom would have done it, but she was never taught to drive as a teenager. Later in life, she was never given the opportunity to drive because the driver's seat was always Dad's "chair."

"Mom, do you really do that?" I asked. "Oh, yes."

"How long have you been giving away candy canes, Mom?"
"Oh, every year. The kids really like them."

"Mom, that is so sweet. What do the kids say when they get one of Aggie's candy canes?"

"Oh, Mark, you know kids, they don't say too much. As long as they pick up the wrappers, that's fine."

"How about the school principal, Mom. What does he say?"
"Oh, Mark, he doesn't say anything."

"Mom, you give out 700 *big* candy canes, and this guy doesn't say a word?"

"Mark, he's kind of a Type A. He's an ass."

Mom rarely uses that kind of language, but she nailed the guy with that one. Once I stopped laughing, I got upset. My mom was giving a candy cane to every kid in the school for eight years in a row, and not only did this principal not say anything, he didn't even notice.

I wanted to drive over to the principal's house and say, "Hi, my name is Mark. My mom, Aggie, gives a big candy cane to every student in your school, and you don't even notice. Mom is right—you are a Type A."

I wanted to do it, but I didn't, because guys like that just don't get it. They wouldn't know a "Nice Bike" if it ran over them. They don't know that when you appreciate others and their contributions that it creates a culture where more people contribute and leave the campsite a bit better than they found it. It helps to create a sense of teamwork within an organization.

When Mom retired from her job, she was sixty-eight years old. She didn't want to quit, but the school district had a policy that all employees must retire by that age. A lame policy, if you ask me. Some people well over sixty years old act like they're in their forties, and some people in their forties act like they're two weeks away from retirement. It's never the age—it's always an attitude.

Well, when the sixth graders at the school heard that Aggie the Candy Cane Lady/Aggie the Retainer Lady was being forced to retire, they were not happy. They knew she loved connecting with them and that she didn't want to quit.

So, the sixth graders started a petition drive to "Save Aggie." Six hundred out of 700 students signed the petition. No doubt the kindergarteners would have signed it, too, if they'd known how to read and write at that point.

The students presented the petition to the school board at a regularly scheduled meeting. Although the board was impressed by the action, they voted to maintain the mandatory retirement policy.

Mom moved on to have lunch with Nubs every day instead of the 700 elementary school children, and the candy cane tradition . . . well, it stopped. No more Hershey's Kisses on birthdays either, and you can bet that quite a few retainers remained in the lunchtime trash bin.

If you go to my parents' home on Washington Memorial Drive, you won't find a lot of awards on the walls. In fact, you won't find any. You'll find the pictures of five children, twelve grandchildren, and a ceramic plaque of *The Last Supper* on the wall. The values are clear in this home.

If you head toward the bathroom, you'll see a set of drawers in the hallway. If you open what used to be the junk drawer, you'll see that the junk has all been cleaned out. The broken crayons, balls of string, collections of odd pens and pencils, random pads of paper, and half-used glue bottles. They're gone.

The drawer is now filled with a neat stack of paper. Each sheet has a heading that reads, "Save Aggie! The Candy Cane Lady," and a collection of signatures is underneath each heading. There are more than 600 signatures from elementary school children for my mom. She connected with each of the students in her lunchroom, and they responded to that connection by acknowledging her generosity, honoring her devotion, and connecting with her kindness.

Dad always had his chair, but Mom had her drawer. Every now and then on a cloudy day, she'd walk over, pull the drawer open a bit, and you could almost hear the love of 600 kids saying, "Nice Bike, Aggie!"

NICE BIKE, *Aggie.*

"Never forget a friend,

and never let a friend forget you."

CHAPTER 17

Traveling with Friends for Life

CONNECTING IS A CONTINUOUS PROCESS. Once you make a connection, you have to nurture it to keep it strong and lasting. You need to keep in touch with people in order to maintain your connection to them, and make sure they stay in touch with you. Give somebody you're connected to a call, send them a book you read, or schedule a time for coffee together—you'll see a return on those connections you invest in.

In my early twenties and fresh out of college, I worked in the marketing department for Jostens, the leading provider of high school class rings, championship rings, graduation regalia, and yearbooks. It was a wonderful job. Jostens' sales representatives use creativity, passion, and dedication to serve their schools. Many of the people I met at Jostens shaped me into the person I am today.

Those who work for this company live in a world of recognizing life's milestones, so it makes sense that they pack their national sales meetings with significant, emotional, and meaningful recognition ceremonies.

At my very first sales meetings, Jostens recognized the sales representative of the year. The honoree was Tom Vosnos who hailed from Chicago. Tom was bigger than life. He was all Greek and extremely proud of his heritage, proud of his family, and a true lover of life.

At the banquet where he received his award, his fellow sales representatives lined up to congratulate him. Tom took extra time with every person, and there were a lot of us. It was his night, and he loved sharing it.

I waited in the back of the line, eager to offer my congratulations. When my moment arrived, I shook Tom's hand and said, "Congratulations, Mr. Vosnos. You are amazing!"

He looked me over and said, graciously, "Thank you, young man. What's your name?"

"Mark Scharenbroich. I'm kind of new with Jostens."

"Oh, sure, I've heard of you," which was doubtful but kind, nonetheless. "It's great to have you as part of the Jostens family. This is such a family business, and you're a part of that family."

"Mr. Vosnos," I pressed him, "if you were to give a young guy one piece of advice, what would it be?"

Tom smiled at me, grabbed me by the lapels of my $79 green plaid sport coat, looked me right in the eyes, and said, "Son, I am going to tell you something: *Never forget a friend, and never let a friend forget you.*"

That was it. I had just received a gift of sage advice from a guy who was at the top of his career. For Tom, every customer, every sales representative, every manager, and every neighbor was a friend. Tom didn't believe in just having friends. He believed in investing in friendships for a lifetime. He connected deeply with everyone who came into his life, and he stayed connected.

NICE BIKE, *Tom Vosnos*

The Winnie Six

How do you view your relationships? Do you wait for people to call, or do you make the first call? Do you make time for people or just wish you had more time? Do you give more than you take? Do you make every connection a positive experience for yourself and others? I'm fortunate. I linked up with a group of five buddies during my high school years, and we have been the best of friends ever since. A key reason for our long-term relationship is the fishing trip we shared in Northern Minnesota during our eleventh grade in high school.

The six of us went to Lake Winnibigoshish. It was so much fun that we decided to do it again the next year . . . and the next . . . and the next. We have passed 50 years of annual trips together and we are still going strong.

We all have nicknames: Chop, Willy, Smoke, Olker, and Dick. My nickname is Nubs, which is short for Norbert, my father's name.

We've shared life's celebrations and life's disappointments. We do our best to remain nonjudgmental, and we are always there for each other—key ingredients to any strong connection. It's a brotherhood. Every year, we look forward to spending one-week fishing at an outpost in Northern Canada. We know we'll be the only ones on the lake, and we'll be fishing from sunup until sundown. It's Nirvana.

We're the Winnie Six, named after Lake Winnibigoshish, where it all began. The week is packed full of traditions, award ceremonies, giggles, stories, twelve-year-old behavior, and some good-natured ribbing. We all have our jobs in camp, from the guy who cleans the fish to the guy who cooks the fish to the guy who cooks the potatoes to the guy who does the dishes to the guy who praises everyone else's efforts.

My wife, Sue, once asked me upon my return, "What do you talk about in the boats during five days of fishing?"

My response was, "Nothing, really."

Sue was puzzled by this. "Nothing?" she asked.

"No, nothing, really. We talk about how our kids are doing, what's new with our wives, how our jobs are going, a few comments on current events, and a couple of references to high school memories. But mostly . . . nothing."

"Five days of nothing," Sue sighed.

"Yeah, that's pretty much it. Nothing . . . I sure do love it."

So, why do I love it? It's sacred time. It's a fact that we're together, and we make the time to be there every year to renew our connection. We're the Winnie Six. In a very real sense, we belong to each other.

We bought a bottle of port in the millennium year of 2000. We were inspired by an old *M*A*S*H* television episode where we learned that Colonel Potter recalled that, during World War II days, he held the rank of private at the time, he and members of his Army unit spent the night in a French château while under fire. They came across a cache of brandy, and proceeded to drink all but one bottle. They made a pledge that the last survivor of the group would get the bottle, and make a toast to his old friends. Years later, Potter turned out to be the last survivor of the group and drank the toast together with his new friends at the 4077th.

We decided to do the same and pass the bottle of port on to the last Winnie guy standing. After a couple of beers around the campfire, we adjusted the plan to share the bottle after the first man leaves the group for the next fishing hole beyond. The thought of one old guy drinking the bottle by himself made no sense.

Our planning for next year's summer trip in July begins on the drive home from the current trip. The annual Winnie Newsletter is sent out in the spring with its usual headline, "If it's the month of May, Winnie isn't far away."

NICE BIKE, *Winnie Six*

The V Club

It all started with Mrs. Wigfield from Gatewood Elementary School in the Hopkins School District in Hopkins, Minnesota. Mrs. Wigfield was recognized as the Minnesota Teacher of the Year, and we were fortunate enough to have all three of our children in her fifth grade classroom.

During our son Michael's year in fifth grade, Mrs. Wigfield and the fifth-grade team came up with the idea of The Decades Project. U.S. history from 1900 to the current year would be taught in sections covering two decades over two weeks. At the end of the lesson, parent volunteers would create an experience to bring events from the two decades alive. Terrific Tuesdays, Wonderful Wednesdays and Fabulous Fridays were devoted to this incredible project that both brought history alive in a compelling manner and included parents in the process.

We signed up with another five couples to host 1930 to 1949. Stephanie Willette and her husband, Brady, were the team captains. A few members of our team observed the first parent-hosted event, a Terrific Tuesday for 1900 – 1929. In my opinion, the first group set the bar way too high! Their day was absolutely incredible. They had a Victorian photographer, a soup line for the Great Depression, a fantastic multi-media show, a vintage Model T parked in front of the school and on and on.

Not that our group of parents was competitive, but the feeling after the first Terrific Tuesday was "Game on!" The twelve parents had several meetings to plan our day, and we were all in. Our documentary media show would have made filmmaker Ken Burns proud. We included a tour of WWII planes in an airplane hangar, issued rationing cards for lunch, and produced a live radio show of "The Shadow" complete with music and sound effects. We included a grandfather who had served in WWII, a grandmother who worked in a factory and represented Rosie the Riveter, and a member from our community who was a Holocaust survivor. Each of the parents dressed as famous people from the decades, including Babe Ruth, Amelia Earhart, and Franklin Roosevelt, who was in a vintage wheelchair. Each character gave a short speech on their lives. I've got to say it was impressive.

After our Fabulous Friday, Steph and Brady invited the parents on our team to their home for a dinner to celebrate our success. We hadn't known each other very well prior to The Decades Project, but the conversation and laughter came easily. We created a real bond.

After dinner, we had a table topic. We went around the table and each of the women told the story about the birth of their child who was now in fifth grade. After the last mom told her story, perhaps it was the wine, but I decided to tell my story about my vasectomy. Trust me, it's a colorful story.

Sure enough, five out of the other six guys went around and told their vasectomy story. Upon the completion of the table talk, we decided to form a club named—what else?—The V Club.

The twelve of us get together several times throughout the year for the Three Ts: triumphs, tragedies, and traditions. From dinners at one of our homes to birthdays, to our kids' high school graduations and weddings, the loss of family members, the birth of grandchildren, an annual hot dish Christmas gathering for the Vs and our kids, the "Vettes," a houseboat adventure in the waters of northern Minnesota. We have laughed together. We have cried together. We are there for each other during the best of times and the worst of times.

None of us were really looking for a new group of friends, and it just grew naturally out of a wonderful volunteer experience and we value the close bond we all have. Our friendship is truly a treasure and a wonderful gift.

NICE BIKE, *Mrs. Wigfield & V-Club*

♥

For the Winnie Six, it's a fishing trip. For the V-Club, it's any excuse to get together. For other people, it's deer camp, a women's weekend, a mastermind group, a bowling league, a book club, the ski trip—same group of friends, same time next year.

So, who is in your group? Who can you turn to? Who could you share your triumphs, tragedies and traditions with over time? Are you investing in your friendships? Are you making connections that help people remember you?

Make a list of the friends you have not heard from in a while and re-connect with them. As Tom Vosnos said, "Never forget a friend, and never let a friend forget you."

"For ages, societies have maintained their cohesion and the connection of the individuals to the community by celebrating important days together."

CHAPTER 18

A Drive to Bean Hole Days

WE ALL WANT AND NEED a connection to a community, whether it's our neighborhood, our place of worship, our school, our business, our family, our country, our world. That's why online social communities have grown so rapidly.

For ages, societies have maintained their cohesion and the connection of the individuals to the community by celebrating important days together. The focus of the celebrations doesn't really matter (and some of them can be pretty weird). It's the celebrations themselves that connect you to a community.

It was the second week of July, and we were standing in line with our three kids and about 3,000 other people waiting for a cup of beans. Baked-in-the-ground beans. If you're a fan of baked beans, these rank right up there in the all-world baked-beans category.

It was the annual Pequot Lakes, Minnesota, population 2285, Bean Hole Days which began in 1938 as a way for the business people in the community to say thank you to the local farmers in the form of a community picnic.

Tradition has it that the beans are made the night before using a closely guarded recipe and placed into large cast-iron pots. Each of the kettles has its own name: Sven, Lena, Ole, Big Bertha and Baby Olga. A hole is dug, a fire is made, and the pots are lowered into the hole to cook overnight. Thus, the title: Bean Hole Days.

After cooking for twenty-four hours, the beans are brought out of the ground and served free, along with a bun and lemonade, to the thousands of people who attend.

Not only are the beans served and eaten, but the King and Queen of Bean Hole Days are crowned, craft booths are lined up, and the ever-popular Three Bobs polka band plays throughout the day. It's kind of a big deal in Pequot Lakes, Minnesota.

Bean Hole Days are fun, kind of campy, and a nice way to connect with neighbors. It's a tradition. It's all about how people need to be a part of something and feel a connection to a community—a town, a wonderful school, an active club, a great company, a thriving association, or an annual event.

Three kinds of events create a sense of community: triumph, tragedy, and tradition.

Triumph: When the team wins the championship, the Apollo 11 lunar module lands on the moon, or the Berlin Wall comes down, people from all walks of life cheer and celebrate the accomplishment together.

Tragedy: When we suffer through a major loss, such as a natural disaster, the attack on 9/11/01 or the loss of a prominent figure, people from a wide range of backgrounds are brought together through this tragic moment.

Tradition: When we celebrate holidays, sing "Happy Birthday," participate in religious ceremonies or wedding rituals, attend an annual sales meeting, or a family reunion, it makes us feel connected, a part of something. Besides, it's fun to shiver with strangers as you watch the annual Winter Carnival parade on the streets of St. Paul, Minnesota during a freezing January day. (Trust me—it's fun!)

So, line up with your neighbors and wait for your cup of baked-in-the-ground beans. Listen as the Three Bobs polka band strikes up a dance tune for the brand-new Bean Hole Days king and queen.

Make a connection with your community.

That day when I drove my rental car through Milwaukee during the Harley-Davidson 100-year anniversary, I was struck by the sense of community the Harley riders shared. They shared a common interest, a pride in belonging to something special, and it was a reason to connect with strangers.

Everyone needs to belong, just like everyone needs to hear "Nice Bike."

NICE BIKE, *Bean Hole Days.*

Make Your Own Traditions

One day, I was catching a flight out of the Meadows Field Airport in Bakersfield, California. As I pulled up to the airport, I noticed a crowd of hundreds of people, news cameras, a fire truck with a huge American flag hanging from the ladder, law enforcement vehicles, and at least thirty Harley-Davidson motorcycles parked nearby.

I walked over to the crowd to see what was going on. It was a homecoming for twenty-three-year-old Army Corporal Wesley Barrientos. Corporal Barrientos was returning home from his third tour in Iraq, this time on two prosthetic legs. He lost both of his legs riding in a Humvee when it was hit by an IED, an improvised explosive device.

Corporal Barrientos's family had expected to see him get off the plane in a wheelchair since he had been fitted with the prosthetic legs only two weeks prior to his homecoming. But he proudly walked over to hug his family and friends.

As Corporal Barrientos walked through the rows of people welcoming him home and saluting him as he passed, a television crew approached, and the reporter approached him.

"Wesley, how does it feel to have a hero's welcome home?"

The corporal smiled and simply said, "I was just doing my job." The local American Legion and VFW members attended in order to offer a salute as he walked by. Cheerleaders and students from his alma mater, Ridgeview High School, turned out to support one of their own. There were also a bunch of Harley-Davidson motorcycle riders, complete with the leather jackets, bandannas, and tattoos, lined up to shout, "Welcome home, Wes!"

I walked over to some of the Harley guys and asked, "Do you know this soldier?"

"Nope," was the answer. "We're not even from Bakersfield." They told me that they were there to honor Corporal Barrientos.

I said, "I understand the local people, the law enforcement, the veterans, but why the Harley riders? What's the connection?"

"Well, this guy served our country, so the least we can do is ride over and welcome him home. A lot of us served in Vietnam, and we never had a welcome home. So, we do this a lot. I guess it's kind of a tradition for us to be there for someone else."

What an example of acknowledging those around you, honoring what's important, and connecting to build community.

NICE BIKE, *Corporal Barrientos and Harley riders*

To make your ride more meaningful and emotion-filled, invest in traditions. A tradition could include interaction with others, celebrating an event, including fun or meaningful symbols, and some type of ritual. Our son Michael and his wife, Kate, enjoy a really cool tradition once a month. (Note: As stated, Michael's wife's name is Kate, our daughter's name is Kate, and our son Matt's wife is named—yep, you guessed it—Kate. We sure love our Kates!)

Michael and Kate live in the port city, Duluth, Minnesota, on beautiful Lake Superior with their three children, Evelyn, James, and Una. There are three climates in Minnesota: cold, really cold, and super cold! Duluth is super cold. On the first weekend of every month, Michael and Kate host a "Jump Club." Anywhere from 15 to 30 people arrive at their home for a potluck meal, then they light a bonfire on the shore, and then they jump into Lake Superior. Not just a quick dip but a full jump in, head under water, swim for a bit, and then jump out.

Keep in mind that the *average* temperature of Lake Superior is 40 degrees Fahrenheit. In January, it is 34 degrees. They love the "Jump Club," as it's a fun get-together with friends, an event people look forward to every month, and their way of saying, *If you are going to live in a cold place, then embrace it and celebrate the outdoors fully.*

Other traditions could be thanking a veteran whenever you see one, taking the time to celebrate a friend's birthday, volunteering at the annual community event, wearing some green on St. Patrick's Day, oohing and ahhing at the Fourth of July fireworks, or dropping off a case of apples at an elementary school for the teachers on their very first day.

Start an annual fishing, camping, shopping, touring, or running event with a group of friends. Create a unique tradition large or small for your family, and do it every week, month, or year—just because it's a tradition.

As Tevye, the main character in Fiddler on the Roof, said, "Because of our traditions, we've kept our balance for many, many years. Here in Anatevka, we have traditions for everything . . . how to sleep, how to eat, how to work, how to wear clothes . . . Without our traditions, our lives would be as shaky as . . . as a fiddler on the roof!"

NICE BIKE, *Jump Club!*

"Go out of your way to connect with the people around you. When they are in need, reach out to them, do something special for them . . ."

CHAPTER 19

Wayside Rests: Benches, Stars, and Holy Cards

NICE BIKE CAN BE EXPRESSED in many different ways, and it's as individual as each one of us. The power of acknowledging, honoring, and connecting can have a remarkable impact that the recipient will remember for a lifetime.

As I mentioned in a previous chapter, I had a long, fun ride with a company called Jostens, the leading provider of yearbooks, class rings, graduation products, and championship rings, and the exclusive provider of rings for Harley-Davidson owners.

The company's entire foundation is based upon helping people celebrate important moments, recognize achievements, and build affiliations. Over the years, I've worked with a lot of wonderful people at Jostens. One of those people was the sales training director, Luke Osterhaus. Luke was a proud son of Iowa. His smile was contagious, his encouragement of others was nonstop, and his devotion to his wife, Jill, and their two daughters was admirable.

Sadly, cancer ended his life at the age of thirty-nine. Luke's legacy continues at Jostens through scholarships in his name, leadership awards given to top performers, and most of all, his spirit for life carried on by so many of the people he touched.

Luke's wife, Jill, notes: "Luke was diagnosed with colon cancer just four months before his life was cut short. In that time, he focused on the simple things that still gave him pleasure in spite of his rapidly declining health and the horrible pain he was experiencing. Prior to the cancer, Luke arose every day by 5:00 a.m. to run his three-mile route hard and fast. He rarely missed a day.

"But as he started feeling sick, he lost the energy to rise early and make the run. Luke's daily run eventually turned into a mile walk. Then, he would just walk down the street a little bit. Every day got more difficult for Luke to find the strength for his short walks."

Jill maintained a website for Luke and wrote about how much he enjoyed walking to the mailbox to pick up the mail. Each day he lost more and more energy and rested for a long time at the mailbox before he ventured back to the house.

The very next morning after the website post, Jill and Luke awoke to find two benches in their yard. Two different groups of friends at Jostens had immediately gone out to buy benches for Luke. Jill set one up in the front yard by the mailbox and one in the backyard.

"When Luke couldn't walk anymore," Jill says, "we would get him out to the benches so that he could just sit and watch the birds. He didn't speak much, but he was at peace taking in all of God's cre ation. A group of Jostens friends had come earlier that month to do a bunch of landscaping work and yard cleanup. The flowers were blooming, and the birds were busy all around. We were surrounded by so many blessings, and he was so overwhelmed by what people had done for him. The benches were just an example of the great friendship and care Luke received from his Jostens family."

Steve Rossi, one of the "bench guys" and an area sales manager for Jostens, added, "We knew how important that daily walk was for Luke, and even with his strength being drained daily, we wanted to support his daily ritual."

They acknowledged his need to be active to the degree he was able, they honored his ritual, and Luke felt one more strong connection with his friends at Jostens. Steve added, "When you practice these three words daily in your actions, you literally change your life and the lives of others." *Acknowledge, honor,* and *connect.*

NICE BIKE, *bench friends.*

The Stars

Years ago, I spoke at Centralia High School in Centralia, Illinois. There were about 1,000 students attending the school, and I remember them as a wonderful audience.

Jack Shelton, the activity director, arranged the program. As I arrived at the school, there was a huge banner over the front door that read, "At Centralia, YOU are a Star!" Walking through the hallways, I noticed paper stars hung all over the walls. Individual names were written on each star. I asked Jack about the banner and the stars, and he said, "It's a project we did last week to build a sense of community in the school. Mark, for the longest time only the athletes got their lockers decorated for games. Theater students never got their lockers decorated for plays, band kids didn't for concerts, so we decided to share the wealth and recognize all of our kids at once."

The student council cut out stars for everyone in the school—students, teachers, cafeteria staff, custodians, and administrators. No one was left out. They wrote the name of each person on his or her individual star. Then, for a couple of weeks, they had a bit of a teaser campaign, saying, "The stars are coming to Centralia!" and telling everyone, "Look for the stars!" It created quite a buzz.

"On star day, we hung a banner that read, *'At Centralia, YOU are a Star!'* on the front door. It was a lot of effort to get more than 1,000 stars taped to the hallways, but it was so rewarding to see the students who had never attended an athletic event, a dance, or a school activity walking down the hallways trying to find their names. Their faces lit up when they saw their very own star."

Jack's favorite story was about one of the senior boys, a student with Down syndrome. He found his name that morning and ran to the office, telling the staff that he had to use the office phone to call his mother.

"Mom, you have to come to school right away! Bring the camera. I will meet you out front!"

Jack said, "He waited at the front of the school and when his mom pulled up in her minivan, he ran out, grabbed her by the hand, and led her down the hallway. When he reached his spot, he said, 'Look, Mom, it's my star!'"

She took his picture and said, "In twelve years, it's the first time he has ever said that he was a star."

It didn't make a difference that there were 1,000 other stars on the wall. This boy's star made a difference to him. He felt acknowledged, honored, and connected.

NICE BIKE, *Jack Shelton and the students of Centralia High School!*

The Holy Card

From grades one to eight, I attended Holy Spirit Catholic Elementary School in St. Cloud, Minnesota. In a town of 40,000 people, we had more than thirteen Catholic elementary schools. St. Cloud is very Catholic. Even the Lutherans are Catholic in St. Cloud. As a kid, we called them "junior varsity Catholics."

My second-grade teacher was Sister Roman, a Franciscan nun. She was the total opposite of the ruler-toting stereotypes you see in the movies. Sister Roman was kind, patient, and an amazing teacher. One of my favorite memories from Holy Spirit was our Friday holy card tradition. If you attended school every day that week, you received the holy card of a Saint as a good attendance award. The Saints played a big part in our Catholic faith, and you prayed to different Saints, depending on their specialty and your need. I mean, Butchers prayed to St. Anthony the Abbot, bakers to St. Nicholas, and beekeepers to St. Ambrose.

If you had a special need, you prayed to a particular Saint for help, such as St. Elmo for abdominal pain, St. Polycarp for earaches, and St. Vitus for snakebites. St. Benedict doubles as the Patron Saint of school children and the Patron Saint for kidney disease, so if you were a second grader with kidney stones, he would be your Saint. Praying to St. Benedict was like having a double indemnity insurance policy.

The holy cards had a nice picture of the Saint on one side and the Saint's special prayer on the other, along with the Saint's feast day, how many people that Saint converted per year, and their lifetime average on conversions. Okay, I'm making up that part about conversions, but they were still like baseball cards for Catholics and pretty darn cool.

Many a Catholic will carry a holy card in a wallet or purse. I always carry my St. Jude, Patron Saint of "lost causes," because you never know when you're going to have a lost cause. It's like the umbrella insurance policy for Catholics.

I missed one day of school that year. It was a Friday, and I was bummed because Sister Roman was passing out the St. Genesius holy card, Patron Saint of actors and the arts. The card had a picture of St. Genesius along with the happy and sad face theater symbol. It was almost as cool as the St. Michael card that featured St. Michael with a sword and snakes.

My mom told me to draw a picture for Sister Roman to show why I missed that day of school. I had a sore throat, so I drew a picture of a cutout section of a throat with a little dwarf pulling levers of a high voice and a low voice, as well as a jar with a frog in it for a "frog in the throat."

I wrote on the top of the page, "To Sister Roman from Mark," and in the other corner, I wrote "JMJ," which stood for Jesus, Mary, and Joseph. We wrote that in the corner of every paper we completed. In fact, to this day, I still write JMJ on my tax forms, it WILL appear somewhere. It was just one more part of growing up Catholic. On Monday morning, I was back at school, and I was excited to give Sister Roman my picture. It was a typical busy second-grade classroom morning. Notes from home were given to Sister Roman, milk money was collected, Todd couldn't get his boots off, Kris and John were fighting over who got to refill the holy water font, and a kid across the hallway had just thrown up.

I brought my picture to Sister Roman. "Here, Sister, I made this picture for you!"

Sister Roman studied the picture, commented on the details, and said, "This is so wonderful. I'm going to keep it forever!"

Now, you know that children hear the words, but they learn from the actions of adults. Instead of putting my picture in the inbox on her desk, Sister Roman reached inside her robes and pulled out a thin black wallet. (I didn't even know nuns carried wallets.)

She very carefully folded the picture that I had made for her, placed it in the wallet, and tucked it back inside her robe.

"Wow!" I thought to myself. "She must have really liked that picture. It must be a pretty good picture. I must be a pretty good artist." Sister Roman had just Nice Biked me.

I will always cherish that moment, but a moment I remember even more is running into Sister Roman four years later. After that year, Sister Roman was assigned to a different school, and she didn't return to Holy Spirit for four years. It was my second day of school as a sixth-grader, and as I was walking down the hall, I felt a tug on the back of my uniform. I turned to see Sister Roman.

"Well, Mark Scharenbroich, look at you! Oh, you've grown! I understand you have Mr. Reed this year, he's an amazing teacher, but you're going to have to work hard! And oh—I almost forgot. I have to share something with you!" At that point, Sister Roman reached into her robes, pulled out a thin black wallet, and carefully unfolded the picture I had made for her four years earlier. I swear on the lives of our three kids!

I was blown away! Now, as you get older, you tend to get a bit more cynical and think, "Does Sister have a filing system back in the convent where she moves pictures from kids in and out of her wallet as she sees them throughout the years? Was this the 'one good idea' she picked up at the staff in-service?"

Maybe she does. But here was an educator who really knew how to acknowledge individual talents, honor our contributions, and connect with us. Like Sister Roman, go out of your way to connect with people around you. When they are in need, reach out to them, do something special for them, even if it's as simple as taping a star on the wall.

NICE BIKE, *Sister Roman.*

"When we contribute, we are making connections—all kinds of connections with all kinds of people."

CHAPTER 20

It's Ninety-One Miles

HOW WE CONNECT WITH OTHERS around us is a choice we make every day. As you take the road to make meaningful connections, there are a few road markers along the way to keep you going in the right direction. It helps to have an inner compass, your road map for the journey, and most of all, the courage to get off the bike and ask others for a little direction.

I pulled my rental car up to the tollbooth on the expressway outside of Tulsa, Oklahoma, and opened my window to pay the toll. An older Southern gentleman was working the booth, and I asked him a question in my quick Minnesota clip.

"Sir, how long does it take to get from here to Fort Smith, Arkansas?"

"Wellllll, I'll tellll you whaaaaat," he responded in a thick and *slow—real* slow— Southern drawl. "It's nahnty-one miles to Fort Smith, Ar-kan-saw. It's up to *yew* how long it's gonna take."

I said thank you a little slower this time, paid my toll, and headed down the road. That gentleman's response kept playing in my head. *It's ninety-one miles, but it's up to you how long it's going to take.*

That older Southern gentleman gave me more than a time frame for my drive that night; he gave me a framework for my life. That might sound like an exaggeration, but the guy had it right. "This is the road of life, kid. It's up to you to decide how you want to travel it." Fast or slow, stopping here or there, or going straight toward my destination. It was all up to me.

Do we have the ability to determine how we want to chart our own journey? Can it really be as easy as deciding how we want to live each day? Is it possible that happiness is a choice? And can being more connected help us live happier lives?

Absolutely.

Do you want to travel down the interstate and go as fast as you can, or do you want to take a few side roads? There are times when you just need to get from point A to point B. To live a full life, however, it's important to slow down every now and then and take a side road, picnic at a wayside rest stop, or connect with a fellow traveler. The side roads of life have some pretty amazing and off-kilter sites: the World's Largest Holstein Cow in New Salem, North Dakota, the World's Largest Peanut in Ashburn, Georgia, and the World's Largest Hairball in Garden City, Kansas. You have the ability to decide how you want to chart your journey.

If you believe that happiness is a choice, then there are some mile markers you can use each day to fuel your journey.

1. See beauty. We have a young friend, Liv Lane, who asked the question, "What happens when you choose to find beauty in your midst each and every day?" Her observation? "Life changes before your eyes." Liv spent a year choosing to see beauty every day by capturing the images and posting them on her social media. She sees beauty through nature, through the eyes of her sons, Ryder and Truman, through the eyes of her husband, Brad, through the eyes of her parents, Pete and Tunie—and even through the eyes of strangers.

Once her radar was up, Liv began to find beauty in the world around her and in the kindness of others. Beauty appears each and every day in the most remarkable ways. Liv is purposeful in *choosing* to see beauty and experiencing happiness even on the worst of days. She stays connected to the beauty in the world around her. Liv intentionally acknowledges the beauty in others and in the ordinary things that most of us fail to notice as we walk through our daily lives.

2. Be forgiving. Some people carry anger and frustration throughout their entire lives. The weight of their anger slows them down and takes the skip out of their step. Some carry big boulders of anger, while others carry anger that's more like an annoying stone in our shoe. It isn't easy to "forgive, let go, and move on," but when we do forgive others and ourselves, it opens our hearts to possibilities and hope. It makes room for us to use that energy toward something a lot more fun and a lot more productive. Plus, medical research has shown that ongoing anger negatively impacts our overall health.

When we let go of anger and bitterness, it becomes much easier to connect with others because we aren't engrossed in our own pain. Think about the last time you were angry with someone. Could you also connect with them in a positive way? Probably not.

3. Contribute something. See for yourself if this is true: The more you give, the more you get. Just try it. Be the first person to say "hello" to a stranger. Pick up a piece of trash you didn't throw down. Buy Girl Scout cookies. Send a thank-you note to one of your former teachers. Attend a high school play and start the standing ovation. Volunteer for Special Olympics. Donate blood. Go beyond yourself and contribute in a way that has meaning for you. Anyone who has served a Thanksgiving meal at a homeless shelter will tell you that the homeless may leave with full stomachs, but the volunteers walk away with full hearts. When we contribute, we are making connections— all kinds of connections with all kinds of people.

4. Show gratitude. Wake up thankful, and go to bed thankful. Appreciate the small wonders that are out there for all of us. Be thankful for family, friends, and the angels who walk among us. Know that there is a reason and a purpose for your life. Appreciate your opportunities, and new doors will open for you every day. Being thankful requires you to acknowledge and honor those things that you are grateful for, and that keeps you more connected to them.

5. Say, "Great!" When people ask how you're doing, don't say, "fine," "doing okay," "all right," "not bad," or "I'd complain, but no one would listen." Those are generic, bland, and not very hopeful answers. Instead, say you're doing "great" no matter what. Here's why:

- It's a reminder that your attitude is your choice.
- It keeps you optimistic and open to possibilities.
- It keeps you moving in the direction you want to go.
- People want to connect with others who are upbeat and hopeful.

Also, think about how you respond when someone says "thank you." We often respond, "No problem." In this case, the emphasis is on the negative word *problem.* Instead, replace "no problem" with "my pleasure" or "happy to help." This positive response is service based and will result in a richer connection with others.

I learned about choosing a positive response from Mr. Leroy Radovich, an industrial arts teacher at St. Cloud Tech High School, home of the fighting Tigers. Mr. Radovich grew up in Hibbing, Minnesota, on what is called the Iron Ore or Mesabi Range. *Mesabi* is an Ojibwa name meaning "giant." The range is a giant area of low rolling hills with a belt of iron ore 110 miles long, averaging one to three miles wide and reaching a thickness as great as 500 feet. Little towns sprang up along the range, and people from this area were known as "Rangers."

Mr. Radovich was indeed a "Ranger" with thick black hair, big bushy eyebrows never properly trimmed, a quick step to his walk, and generous splashes of Old Spice. He loved who he was and what he did. One day, he called me out in the hallway by his classroom.

"Hey, Mark Scharenbroich, come here!"

"Yes, Mr. Radovich?"

"How you doing today?"

"I'm fine," I replied.

"Fine? *FINE?* Is that the best you got? Did you think that one through? Hey, look at me. Ask me how I'm doing? Go ahead, ask me!"

I asked sheepishly, "How are you doing Mr. Radovich?"

"I'm doing great!" he roared. "You know why? Because I thought it through! Every day I wake up, I look in the mirror and say, "Good morning Mr. Radovich!" Then I ask myself a question, 'Mr. Radovich, what kind of day do you want to have today? A fine day, OK day, average day, bad day? How about great? You know why? Because great is better than fine you pickle head! It's a choice! It's not where you start in life; it's where you end up! OK, let's try it again, Scharenbroich, how are you doing?"

"Great," I managed to squeak out.

"Good! Now get out of here!" bellowed Ranger Radovich.

I never had the guy for a class. I never even wanted the guy for a class! I thought he was nuts. But to this day, I never use the word fine when asked how I'm doing. When I was sixteen years old, Leroy Radovich planted an acorn in me that has matured into an oak tree. He knew what mattered, and he left a huge legacy for all those he connected within the halls of Tech High School.

NICE BIKE, *Mr. Radovich.*

What path will you take? How will you choose to connect to the world around you? Knowing where you want to go and how you want to get there is key to a successful journey. It's ninety-one miles to Fort Smith, Arkansas. And it's up to you how long it's going to take.

NICE BIKE, *Tollbooth Guy.*

"Clearly articulated core values
and beliefs, along with a strong moral compass,
are what build a solid foundation."

CHAPTER 21

Get Out Your Compass

I WAS BORN IN A BASEMENT HOUSE. That sounds like the start of a country western song or something you tell your kids about how tough it was "in my day." But it's the truth. And looking back, it was a great life lesson on how important a good foundation is to your journey.

You see, my dad was one of those veterans who came home after World War II to find a career, buy a home, and start a family after surviving the war.

Taking out a large mortgage to build a home was not a way of life for most of his generation, and my parents did what a lot of people in our neighborhood did: They built our house by digging a basement and putting a flat roof over that foundation. We lived there until we saved enough money to add a first floor and complete the rest of the home.

The basement house had a small kitchen, one bedroom, living room, bathroom, and a utility room with small windows that didn't let in much light. With four small children and my folks living in that small basement house, it made for a really long Minnesota winter.

To keep costs low, it was common for family and friends to help each other build the upper part of their houses. Thank goodness, my dad and his friends finished the upper part of the house shortly after I was born.

Looking back, the basement house idea has a lot of merits. My parents always believed in living within their means. All of us should start with a strong foundation.

It seems that with today's easy access to loans and credit cards, a lot of people start with the penthouse first, take on too much debt, and get in way over their heads. The same can be said for accumulating material things. A lot of people buy stuff to impress other people: "Hey, look at my stuff! Pretty cool, huh?" Meanwhile, their possessions are all resting on a pretty weak foundation.

How many times have you watched a news story about a natural disaster where someone's home is destroyed by a flood or tornado? It seems that every time the newsperson asks the homeowners how they're doing, the answer is usually: "We all got out okay. Everyone survived. We can always rebuild. We can replace our things, but as long as we have our family, we'll be okay."

Having a strong foundation is about knowing what's important, what matters, and what lasts. Clearly articulated core values and beliefs, along with a strong moral compass, are what build a solid foundation. Individuals, organizations, and companies with a strong foundation based on sound principles and values will thrive during tough times.

Can you clearly articulate your core values? Can you make tough decisions based on your inner compass? What is your foundation built on? As Roy Disney said, "When your values are clear to you, making decisions becomes easier."

Your Core Beliefs

Having an inner clarity centered in core beliefs that are guided by a sense of purpose and pursued with integrity and passion is your best foundation for building meaningful connections in the best and worst of times.

It's not about having a lot of rules but rather a simple set of principles that will show you the way. This is especially true in business, and many of us have experienced exceptional customer service firsthand with companies like Nordstrom, Starbucks, or Southwest Airlines. That service is based on their core values.

However, the importance of core values is also evident in other areas. I am certain this is true in education. I once spoke to the educators of South High School in Plainfield, Illinois. The principal was Dan Goggins. When I asked Dan how I could serve him and his staff, I expected the usual: "Well, just motivate them, you know, fire them up." I was surprised when I heard Dan say, "Mark, we have four core values that we base all of our decisions on:

1. Kids come first. Any action must be good for kids and improve student achievement. If so, the answer is yes.

2. Great teachers make great schools. Teachers must take responsibility for student learning. Staff collaboration is the key to our success.

3. Relationships are vital. We need staff members connected to staff members, staff members connected to students, and staff members connected to the community.

4. Celebrate diversity and promote respect. We need to connect the dots with everyone in our school community.

Dan added, "If you ask any of our staff members what our core values are, they can cite each one and why it is vital to our success. Tie into one or all of our core values and you will hit a home run."

This is also true in parenting. Our three children are all now in their 30s, and we are extremely proud of the choices they have made and the adults they have become. When they were growing up, Sue and I didn't have a lot of rules or road maps. There were very clear lines drawn in the sand on drugs, alcohol, and sexuality—and we stuck to three basic principles to keep a happy home:

1. Pick up after yourself. If you took it out, put it back. It's your room, seat in the car, place at the table, so leave it better than how you found it.

2. Put one in for the team. If you see a dish that needs to be put away, a trash can that needs to be emptied, a phone that needs to be answered, put one in for Team Scharenbroich. Contribute your time, energy, and talent for the good of all those around you.

3. Be happy. If you sense unhappiness, add joy. Smile. Be appreciative.

The kids connected with these three guidelines. Their rooms stayed reasonably clean, they learned the value of contributing, and they gained the power to choose their own well-being.

Some of the best organizations I have worked with have an uncanny similarity to the guidelines we set as parents. I recommend these three core values for any organization, especially a business.

1. Pick up after yourself. Take responsibility for your actions. Own it.

2. Put one in for the team. Find ways to support others. Go beyond what's expected.

3. Choose a good attitude. Bring some joy to the workplace.

A lot of organizations come up with so many policies that the end result is to make everything complex and complicated. Yet, the best organizations run by doing the very basic things exceptionally well.

One of our favorite stops on a drive to our cabin is an independent fast food restaurant called Happy's Drive-In. They serve tasty hamburgers, hot dogs, and ice cream. However, they are really known for living up to their name. The teenagers working at Happy's truly are happy. They are genuine and enthusiastic, and they delight in serving others.

I asked the owner of Happy's how he created and maintained such a great attitude with his team. He said, "We work hard to hire kids who are friendly, and we just ask them to have fun with our customers and each other. In fact, when a crew member walks in the back door for work, everyone turns and yells hello to the person. If they don't say hello back in a cheerful manner, the kids make them go back out the door and come back in happier. It's silly, but it works." The core value at Happy's Drive-In? *Be happy.*

Nice Bike is not complicated. It's being more aware of others through acknowledgment. It's being more interested in others by honoring their story. It's making a connection with others through validation.

NICE BIKE, *Principal Goggins and the happy team at Happy's Drive-In.*

It's More Than a Box

I spoke at a company meeting for PCA (Packaging Company of America), a manufacturer of container board and corrugated packaging. You might expect "We make boxes" to be the first statement that pops up on their website, but instead, it says: "A company focused on People, Customers, Trust."

PCA has 8,350 employees with $6.6 billion in net sales. That's a lot of boxes. PCA is the fourth largest container producer and is growing, but it's not because their products are less expensive than their competitors'. PCA is growing because:

1. They over-deliver quality products, services, and ideas.
2. They stay connected to their customers and build strong, long-term relationships.
3. The behavior of their people is judged against the ultimate standard: The Golden Rule. Treat people like you want to be treated.

It's easy to sell a product that has more bells and whistles, but thriving in a commodity business through clear core values is impressive. Plus, everyone I worked with at PCA had a positive, upbeat attitude. They have a strong culture built on a solid foundation of real service. The team at PCA not only knows their three core values, but they live them every day.

NICE BIKE, *Packaging Corporation of America.*

Know What Matters

To understand a strong foundation for life, go to any retirement center and visit for a while with the older people who are in the final years of their journey. Look at their rooms, and see what's on their walls. You won't see pictures of cars, boats, or jewelry. You'll see pictures of children, grandchildren, great-grandchildren—because these elders have learned that the best things in life are not things, but people.

What really matters the most to you? Build your foundation for living first based on what you value most, and then move up.

A wonderful perspective on strong foundations comes from one of my boyhood sports heroes, Minnesota Twins baseball player Harmon Killebrew. Harmon played professional ball from 1954 to

1975. He hit a total of 573 home runs and eight times in his career, he hit more than 40 home runs during a single season. He became one of the American League's most feared power hitters of the 1960s.

As a kid, I spent a lot of Sundays sitting in the backyard, watching my dad grill chicken while we listened to the Twins game on WCCO-AM radio. Harmon was everyone's favorite when I was growing up. You might take some other ball player's baseball card and attach it to the wheels of your Schwinn bike with clothing pins to simulate the sound of a motorcycle, but not Harmon's. His baseball card went on the shelf.

In 1984, Harmon Killebrew was the very first Minnesota Twin to be inducted in the Major League Baseball Hall of Fame. I listened to his speech, broadcast live on WCCO. He spoke of the times he and his brother played baseball in the backyard of his farm in Idaho. Once, their mother called to the boys to stop sliding because they were tearing up the grass. The boys' father walked over and said, "Mother, we're raising boys, not grass. Let them slide." His father recognized what really mattered. What a great foundation!

What are your core values? What's important to you? What really matters?

Sometimes the smallest actions and the simplest rules can have the biggest impact. Figure out the three rules you live by, and the rules you want your family and business to live by. Determine who you are and where you are. Find your moral magnetic north and set a course along your chosen path. Set your foundation, and build connections from there. The road to making meaningful connections starts with a strong foundation.

NICE BIKE, *Harmon Killebrew.*

"Open it."

CHAPTER 22

Two Words from Aggie

SOME OF THE GREATEST LESSONS IN LIFE come from adults who share keen insights when we are at a young age. Advice from parents, grandparents, an aunt or uncle or a significant adult can remain in our hearts and minds forever. These insights guide us in making good decisions or finding our way when we get lost.

Classic advice from some of these wise sages are:

"Little stuff matters; manners will get you a long way."

"Don't quit until tomorrow."

"Never spend money you don't have."

"Eat with your mouth closed."

"Always ask; they can only say no."

"If it sounds too good to be true, it usually is."

"If it was easy, everyone would do it."

"Failure is not fatal. Learn the lesson, then get back up and try again."

"If you are going to do something, do it right."

"Everyone is struggling in some way, so try to be kind."

The list is endless.

The advice isn't always earth-shattering or life-changing, sometimes the smallest suggestions just stick with you. As we would finish an assignment at Holy Spirit Elementary School, we would raise our hand and say, "I'm done!" Sister Rose Margaret would come back with, "Cakes are done, people are finished." When we asked the question, "Can I go to the bathroom?" Sister's response was, "I am sure you can, but the real question is, 'May I go to the bathroom.' I shared those same words with our children. Of course, my kids gave me the same look that I am sure we gave Sister Rose Margaret.

Of course, there is also my Aunt Nina. She lived in Washington, D.C., and was a world traveler. If there was any sophistication in our family, Aunt Nina had it all. When Aunt Nina and Uncle Bernie traveled from Washington, D.C., to St. Cloud, Minnesota, for a family visit, it was a big deal. We even had a spread of fancy hors d'oeuvres set out prior to dinner: meatballs, deviled eggs, pigs in a blanket plus chips and Philly cream cheese onion dip. I remember loading up a potato chip with lots of dip when Aunt Nina came up behind me and said, "Young Markie, it's called a dip not a shovel. Just dip the chip." To this day when I grab a chip and dive into the dip I can hear Aunt Nina's voice, "Young Markie . . ." That said, I still use the chip as a shovel every now and then.

Sage Advice

Whenever I hear people quote sage advice from an elder, I wonder, "What advice have I given that my children or grandchildren will remember?" I am honestly not sure. Plus, I am almost afraid to ask — wondering if I could have guided more or given more. I would hope that I have taught them to leave the campsite better than how they found it. To be respectful to all regardless of their title or their background. That it's important to be interested in others and to be curious. Don't leave wet towels on the floor, please hang them up. To pursue their passion no matter where it takes them. Most of all, to call their mother.

I look back at my parents and reflect on the advice they shared with me. The guidance I received from my father, Norbert, included, "Never whittle a stick with the knife coming towards you; always cut away from you." "Carry at least five dollars with you at all times." "Keep your elbows off the dinner table, and by the way, take your hat off, this isn't a barn." All the other lessons were pretty much taught by example, not by words.

My mother, Agnes, shared the same advice that her father had given her: "Be kind. Do things for people, expecting nothing in return." "Support yourself. Pay your own way." Along with that my mother added, "Don't get a big head. Be humble." "Laundry hung outside on the clothes line just smells better; it's worth the effort." "Why pay full price when you can use a coupon?" Again, all the other insights were taught by example versus words.

However, during mom's last days, she gave me the greatest gift of all, two words that have guided me better than any other . . . and they weren't *Nice Bike.*

After my father's passing, mom stayed in the home they had built more than 60 years ago. Mom took care of everything from her garden to her laundry to cutting the grass and raking the leaves. Mom stayed active and even walked on her treadmill at age 96. Although she suffered from painful arthritis in her hands, she continually hand-stitched quilts for her family, grandchildren, and friends. Mom said, "When you stop trying, you give up, and I'm not ready to give up just yet." Her spirits were always positive, and she constantly had a steady stream of visitors every day. She made everyone she knew feel like they were her favorite child, grandchild, niece, nephew, neighbor, or friend. We all thought, "I am Aggie's favorite."

In early October, Mom was raking leaves, and she got really tired. This was a woman who never took a nap. She got up early and stayed up late. However, Aggie had a nagging cough that continued throughout the summer. She was finally convinced to see the doctor. Sure enough, Mom had pneumonia, and she just couldn't shake it. Her lungs were filling with fluid and, following an Emergency Room visit, doctors removed some of the fluid filling her lungs to help with her breathing. Upon testing, they discovered that she had lung cancer.

Her doctor explained her options and after one night in the hospital, Aggie decided to go home, both figuratively and literally. From the time she was diagnosed until the time of her passing, three short weeks slipped by before we said goodbye to our mother. It was a peaceful, loving, and graceful journey for Aggie in her own home, in her own bed with her family at her side. May we all live to be 97 and say goodbye in the same way.

My wife, Susan, and I cared for mom during her last three nights. When we were kids, mom always had set routines for us, and she treasured her own routines as well. First, Susan gave her the glaucoma drops. The doctor told her a long time ago to make sure that she took her glaucoma drops every night, so that had to be first.

Second, mom turned to me and said, "Mark, take out my hearing aid." As I did, she added, "Open it." I asked back, "Open it, Mom?" She replied, "Yes, open it. It saves the batteries." Knowing that she was looking at a short time on this earth, she still wanted to save those batteries. You can purchase a 12 pack of those batteries at Walgreens for $9.95, but as Mom instructed, I opened it.

Third, when we were kids, as Mom tucked us in for the night she always said, "Tell me about the good things that happened today." So, we asked Mom the same. "Mom, tell us about all the good things that happened today." Of course, the answer was all about the family and friends who came to see Aggie during her final days. This included the young woman who remembered Aggie from her days as an elementary school cafeteria monitor. She said, "Aggie, I always had you open my milk cartons for me at lunch. I knew I could do it by myself, but I loved it when you did it for me."

Fourth, every night when we were children, before Mom kissed us goodnight, she said the Angel Prayer with us. "Angel of God, my guardian dear, to whom God loves, commits me here. Ever this night be at my side to light and guard, to rule and guide. Amen."

Mom always let us know that the angels were there with us every night. So, we recited the Angel Prayer with mom.

We followed a kiss goodnight with "We love you, Mom."

On Mom's last day, she started to go on the journey. Her eyes were closed most of the day, and she didn't speak that much. She was at peace. That night we followed the same routine, knowing that it is what Mom would have liked. At the end of a tearful, "Good night, Mom, we love you," Susan, the "compliance officer," asked "Mark, did you take out your mom's hearing aid." Oops, I forgot.

I went over to Mom's bedside and said, "Mom, I forgot to get your hearing aid. I am going to remove it now." With that, Mom's eyes opened, she looked at me and whispered, "Open it."

My mother's last words to me were, "Open it." I was hoping for, "You've always been my favorite" or "There is a box in the closet . . . share it with your brothers and sister . . . ." No, instead Mom whispered, "Open it."

Early the next morning, with her family surrounding her and with my younger brother John holding her hand, Mom was peacefully guided by the angels all the way home.

Since Mom's passing, there hasn't been a day that has gone by that I haven't reflected on the gift of those two beautiful words: "Open it." Next to birth, it is the greatest gift Mom could have ever given to me. The void created by my mom's passing was comforted by this sage advice. It captured the essence of my mom's life.

"Open it," which means to me: Don't waste. Don't take for granted. Take care of things. Take care of each other. Be open and kind to others. If you want to connect with others, open it. Open your heart to who you are and how to love fully. See and embrace the simple joys of life. They are a gift. They are right in front of you . . . "Open it."

NICE BIKE, *Mom.*

"Acknowledge, honor, connect,

and you will change the world,

one person at a time."

CHAPTER 23

The Ultimate Nice Bike

FROM READING MY STORIES, and learning about my friends, family, and business associates, I hope that you have gotten a clear understanding of what Nice Bike is all about. Using these two words provides the fuel to transform your organization and your life. Nice Bike will enable you to acknowledge, honor, and connect with those around you. Sometimes, all three happen at once. This is the real magic of Nice Bike.

My dad worked hard at the post office every day sorting mail. He was proud to be a part of the United States Postal Service. He always griped that UPS delivered boxes and "took the cream off the top." Dad said, "Anyone can deliver boxes. Try sorting and delivering a couple of million Christmas cards every year, and we'll see what they can do!"

Like a lot of dads of that era, he was always there for us, never missing a ball game or a school event. Unlike some dads I've seen at my kids' ball games, my dad never yelled at the referees, complained to the coach about my playing time, or told the coach what play to run in a game. Win or lose, the most Dad would ever say was "good game." I think this is a great lesson for parents. Support the child, and simply enjoy the game.

Dad and I didn't do a lot of things together. We never threw a baseball back and forth. We never overhauled a '57 Chevy or built a tree fort in the backyard. We went fishing once and hunting once. I remember both clearly, especially the pheasant hunting trip in Minnesota. I was twelve years old. We pulled up to a farmer's field with a long ditch next to the road. Dad said, "Yeah, Mark, you go down to the ditch and kick around. If any birds flush, you hit the ground real quick." At that point, I wished that we had owned a dog. Dad and I did watch a lot of WWII movies together. He liked to watch these since he served in that war, so we would sit on the couch and watch them on our black-and-white television. Plus, if a first-run movie about the war was showing at the Paramount Theater in downtown St. Cloud, we jumped in the Ford to see it. To this day, I have a huge interest in WWII history because of the seed that Dad planted.

Love was displayed daily in how our parents were there for us—by working hard, caring for us, reading us bedtime stories, making sure we said our prayers, having great meals as a family every night at the table, and making a big deal out of holidays.

Love was popcorn and a soda pop on Saturday night. Love was slipping me an extra two dollars when I went out on a Friday night. Love was packing the family in the Ford and visiting the relatives for the day or taking a Sunday drive with a stop at the Dairy Queen for an ice cream cone at the end of the drive.

It was the little things that displayed love in our house. Dad loved being in the bowling league with his buddies. He bowled every Wednesday night, and when we woke up for school on Thursday morning, there would always be five bags of Old Dutch garlic potato chips on the kitchen table—one bag for each kid.

In our house, love was demonstrated by Mom's hard work. I would play in the swamp not too far from our house and come home covered in mud. Mom just grabbed the garden hose, sprayed the mud off my jeans (while I was wearing them), and washed the jeans that night. Mom fixed the flats on our bike tires, typed our handwritten school papers, sewed our clothing, and pretty much ran the home without ever complaining or whining about any of it.

My parents balanced our upbringing with demonstrated love and clear boundaries. The boundaries were set curfews, church every Sunday, and proper behavior at the dinner table, such as our always asking, "May I be excused?" before leaving the table. Rules and guidelines were clear and enforced.

But as much as we were loved, we never shared the words "I love you." It's not that we didn't feel it; we just didn't say it. I don't think we even said "I like you" that much. As an adult, I heard a speaker by the name of Leo Buscaglia, the author of *Living, Loving and Learning.* Buscaglia encouraged his listeners to tell the people who mean the most to them—especially their parents—how much they're loved. That one really hit me because, I realized I had never shared those words with my parents. I said, "I love you," to my wife and children daily, but I had never said it to my parents.

I don't know why, but it wasn't easy to say it to Mom and Dad. The words should have flowed out of me, but it was difficult to tell my parents—out loud—that I loved them. I saved the moment for Christmas Eve, which was always my parents' favorite night of the year. The rest of the family was in the kitchen, and Dad was in the living room sitting in his chair.

"Dad, do you have a moment?" I asked. "Ya," he replied.

"Well, Dad, it's just that you never missed a game I played, and you never yelled at the refs or talked to the coaches, and we did go hunting that one time . . . and . . . well, I . . . uh . . . I love you, Dad."

"Good. Tell your Mother."

That pretty well covered it. Granted, it got easier after that first time, and before long, every conversation ended with "I love you, Dad" and a quick return of "Love you, too, Son."

I knew a lot about my parents, Nubs and Aggie, but not as much as I should have known. Like a lot of kids, I took a lot for granted and never looked for heroes in my own home until I got older. A turning point for me was in the 1980s when I attended the funeral of a friend's parent. He had lost his other parent about a year earlier. His advice given to me in the funeral home really hit home: "Hey, buddy, ask your folks some questions."

"What do you mean?" I asked.

"The little stuff that you can never know once they're gone. How they met, where they honeymooned, who their favorite teacher was, what their first job was, what their favorite book was . . . the little stuff that captures who they were. Once your parents are gone, the library is closed."

That statement really got to me. So, I started asking my parents some questions. I knew my mom had grown up on a farm in Eden Valley, Minnesota, but I didn't know that she had gone to school in a one-room schoolhouse for eight years with thirty-five other kids, or that Grandma Anna was one of the first teachers at that same school. As a young teacher, Anna boarded in a room at a local farmhouse where she met a young farmer named Jim whose family owned the house. They married a year later.

I knew that my dad had served in the Navy in WWII. I can't tell you how many Saturday mornings I spent at the local VFW (Veterans of Foreign Wars) club. On Saturday morning, I would go grocery shopping with my mom and dad. As soon as we hauled in the last bag of groceries and placed them on the kitchen table, Dad would turn to Mom and say, "Aggie, I'm going to the VF."

VF was short for VFW. Why Dad had a need to abbreviate that

one, I don't know.

"Well, Nubs," Mom would say, "if you're going to the VF, at least take the boy with you."

You see, I was the fourth born in a family of five kids, and I was the youngest child for ten glorious years before my younger brother, "Oops," was born. (Actually, his name is John, and he turned out to be the crown prince of the family.)

Dad would drive me to the VFW, and he'd always order a Grain Belt beer on tap while I had my favorite, a bottle of Orange Crush. All of the guys would be there: Ron Gruber, Leo Satzer, Lenny Keller, Cliff Eisenreich, Bud Streitz, and Woody Bisset. To me, these men were bigger than life. They always made me feel welcome as I sipped my Orange Crush and listened to them talk.

But as a kid, I never knew that these were the same guys who served in WWII. I didn't know that these were the men who attacked Omaha Beach on D-Day. I didn't know that these were the men who froze in the foxholes and held on during the Battle of the Bulge. I didn't know that these were the men who hit the volcanic sand of Iwo Jima or survived the Bataan Death March. I never knew, because they never talked about the war. Never.

They talked about their families, their work, or the Vikings and the Twins. They spent one entire Saturday morning discussing the art of properly sealing a toilet with a wax ring, complete with illustrations on a bar napkin. But they never talked about their war experiences.

Once I finally started to ask the right questions, I discovered that my dad had served on the aircraft carrier USS Lexington. He flew with a crew of two other men in a plane called the TBF Avenger, a torpedo bomber. The crew was made up of a pilot, a turret gunner, and a radioman/ventral gunner (under the tail), which was used to defend against enemy fighters attacking from below and to the rear. Dad served as the radioman/ventral gunner. His crew landed on the deck of the *Lexington* ninety-seven times in training and combat missions.

"The very first time we landed on the *Lex*," Dad told me, "the seas were rough, and the ship was heaving up. We came in too fast, and we hit so hard that it blew out the tires on the plane."

"What did you think at that moment, Dad?" I asked him. "I thought it was going to be one long war."

Dad's hometown newspaper, the St. Cloud Daily Times, carried this paragraph in 1945 about their hometown son: "Norbert Scharenbroich, ARM1c, home on leave, is a crewman of air group 30, which destroyed or damaged 219 Japanese aircraft and 51 ships during five months combat aboard an aircraft carrier in the Pacific, at a loss of three pilots killed and five wounded."

Dad kept a journal during part of the war that I found after his death. He wrote warmly about turret gunner A. L. "Jonesy" Jones, ARM2c from Florida and Lieutenant E. C. Knospe from St. Paul, who was the pilot and "a good egg." Dad had entries for almost every day up until they did a bombing run on the island of Truk in the Pacific. On the return from their bombing run, they had to ditch in the ocean, and the pilot died in the water. Dad's last entry was: "This is a very grim business." After that, he had put the pen down, closed the journal, and put the journal into a box not to be discovered until after his passing.

A Plane Ride with Dad

"What did you do after the war, Dad?" I asked him once.

He was matter of fact. "I came home to St. Cloud, got a job, and then married your mother."

When I pried a bit more, he told me, "I haven't been in a plane since I flew home from Pearl Harbor."

"Dad, you haven't flown since the war? Why?"

"Oh, you know your mother," Dad said. "She never wants to go anywhere."

I'm on a flight almost weekly due to my speaking career. So I invited my dad to take a trip with me to Washington, D.C. I was giving a big speech. In fact, I was sharing a stage with the First Lady. Well, she spoke the day before me, but it was *the same stage!*

I begged my mother, "Please, Mom, make the trip with us."

But she couldn't be persuaded. "No, Mark. I just don't want to go. Take your father, and do me a favor."

It was a great trip. My dad enjoyed my presentation, and we toured the city together. The last monument we planned to visit was the Lincoln Memorial. We ended up there late in the evening. Other than Abraham Lincoln, it was just my father and me standing there that night. It was a very powerful moment when we sensed the greatness that this country was built on.

We left the Lincoln Memorial around 11:00 p.m. and took a left along the Mall. In just a short time, we came upon the Vietnam Veterans Memorial. The first thing that came to my mind was the number 256. That was my lottery draft number from the Vietnam War.

A lot of men volunteered to serve, and a lot of men were drafted to serve. The lottery involved 365 blue plastic capsules, each containing one date for the calendar year, that were dumped into a large container. The capsules were drawn out one at a time and assigned sequentially rising numbers. If your birthday corresponded to a low number, you were sent to Vietnam. If you had a high number (like 256), you weren't drafted, which meant that men served in our place.

For those who served and lost their lives in Vietnam, 58,178 names are engraved in polished black granite on the Vietnam Veterans Memorial. The first American soldier killed in the Vietnam War was Air Force T-Sgt. Richard B. Fitzgibbon, Jr., and the last was Kelton Rena Turner, an eighteen-year-old Marine. He was killed in action on May 15, 1975, two weeks after the evacuation of Saigon.

With the exception of the return of our prisoners of war, those who returned from their service in Vietnam weren't welcomed home with parades. Unlike the WWII returning soldiers, they received no fanfare: there were no cheering crowds of people or banners hung throughout their towns. They were not acknowledged, honored, or thanked. When I ask Vietnam veterans to tell me about the toughest part of the war, many of them say it was coming home.

As my dad and I were walking beside the memorial wall, we noticed two Vietnam vets standing close to it. They were wearing their Army jackets and silently staring at the engravings of the names of their fellow soldiers. My dad slowly walked over to the two men and said, "Excuse me. Were you fellows over there . . . Vietnam?"

"Yeah. Yeah, we were," said one of the men.

After a long pause, my dad said, "Thank you, fellows. Welcome home."

"Sir, you are the very first person who has ever said thank you to me for serving my country. That means a lot, man."

At that point, the Vietnam vet moved closer to my dad and gave him a big bear hug. Then the other Vietnam vet did the same. My dad was not known as a hugger, but totally out of character, he gave a big hug back to each man. I noticed tears in the eyes of the Vietnam veterans and in the eyes of the WWII veteran, my father. That was the first and last time I ever saw my father cry.

Dad acknowledged the Vietnam vets, honored their service, and connected with them on a very personal level. It's a moment I will always cherish. I didn't know it at the time, but it was the ultimate Nice Bike.

Acknowledge, honor, connect, and you will change the world, one person at a time.

NICE BIKE, *Dad.*

The next time . . .

The very next time you see a Harley-Davidson biker roaring down the road, use it as a reminder to turn to the person next to you and say "Nice Bike" to him or her. You might be in a family vehicle or on public transportation. Find out what's important to whoever's traveling with you, and make a connection that matters. *Acknowledge* how important they are to you, *honor* them by knowing what's important to them, and make a meaningful *connection* with them.

"Hey, Nice Bike!"

Over the next 30 days, I pledge to:

ACKNOWLEDGE . . .

To be more aware of others. Have my radar up. Focus on the changes I need to embrace for growth. Work at being more interested than interesting. Learn how to stop, drop, and listen.

HONOR . . .

To know what's important to myself and more importantly, to others. Replace the words "No problem" with "My pleasure." Choose to respond with "Great" instead of "Just fine." To increase my passion to serve others. Become more fully engaged in my relationships.

CONNECT . . .

To be appreciative. Say thanks more often and more authentically. Take action to make the call, send the e-mail, write the note, share the words, take the time to connect with others.

Each week I will *Nice Bike* a colleague, a client, a family member, a neighbor, and a stranger.

MAKING MEANINGFUL CONNECTIONS
ON THE ROAD OF LIFE

ABOUT THE AUTHOR

MARK SCHARENBROICH is a keynote speaker and humorist based in Minneapolis, Minnesota. He has never ridden on a Harley but he and his wife, Susan, do own a pontoon boat. He has earned an Emmy award, and his video programs have received a Silver Screen, Golden Apple, Telly, and International Health and Medical film awards. He has also been inducted into the National Speakers Association's prestigious Hall of Fame and named as one of the top 30 motivational speakers by Global Gurus. He was featured in the 1981 Jostens film, *The Greatest Days of Your Life . . . (so far),* which was viewed by millions of high school students in the 1980s. Mark speaks internationally to associations, business groups, and educators. Visit Mark Scharenbroich online:

NiceBike.com • Mark@nicebike.com